COLLECTING ANTIQUE

Stickpins

identification & value guide

Jack and Elynore "Pet" Kerins

COLLECTOR BOOKS
A Division of Schroeder Publishing Co., Inc.

ON THE COVER

Left to right

TURQUOISE AND SNAKE • Yellow gold pin and mount with a snake coiled around an oval cabochon turquoise, snake's head is set with a 2mm mine-cut diamond, late Victorian era. $135.00–175.00.

PEAR • Yellow gold pin and mount with an opal pear dangling from a branch with green basse-taille enameled leaves, late Victorian era. $135.00–175.00.

INTAGLIO • Yellow gold pin and engraved gold mount set with an oval carnelian carved in the left profile of an ancient warrior, late Victorian era. $100.00–150.00.

CAMEO • Yellow gold pin and oval mount with the left profile of a Roman lady carved in sardonyx, late Victorian era. $350.00–500.00.

MEMORIAL • Yellow gold pin and marquise-shaped mount bordered by eight flat-cut rhodolite garnets and 12 seed pearls surrounding a crystal cover encasing plaited brown hair, circa 1820. $400.00–500.00.

OPAL CRESCENT • Yellow gold pin with a white and yellow gold mount set with a crescent-shaped opal, late Victorian era. $400.00–500.00.

WOLF • Yellow gold pin and mount shaped in the head of a wolf set with rose-cut ruby eyes and a pearl in its mouth, pin is marked "14K" and hallmarked with an arrowhead surrounding the letter "C" (Carter, Gough & Co., Newark, N.J.), circa 1915. $125.00–175.00.

Centered at bottom

MASK • Yellow gold pin and mount with a mask shaped from jet and set with two 2mm mine-cut diamond eyes, late Victorian era. $65.00–100.00.

Searching For A Publisher?

We are always looking for knowledgeable people considered experts within their fields. If you feel that there is a real need for a book on your collectible subject and have a large comprehensive collection, contact us.

COLLECTOR BOOKS
P.O. Box 3009
Paducah, Kentucky 42002-3009

Book layout: Karen Geary
Cover design: Beth Summers

Additional copies of this book may be ordered from:

COLLECTOR BOOKS
P.O. Box 3009
Paducah, KY 42002-3009

@ $16.95. Add $2.00 for postage and handling.

DEDICATION

To my father, John Joseph Kerins (1889–1953), who prior to World War I and during the "Roaring Twenties" owned and wore five stickpins that eventually became the inspiration for Pet's collection.

DAD'S STICKPINS
(Left to Right)

SYNTHETIC RUBY • On a Tiffany type gold-plated mount and pin.
CONVERTED COIN • U.S. gold piece, polished and engraved: "K."
FLEUR-DE-LIS • 10K gold pin and mount set with amethyst.
SIGNET • 10K gold pin and mount with engraved initials, "JK."
SYNTHETIC EMERALD • On Tiffany type gold-plated mount and pin.

Their total market value: $175.00–250.00 — Their personal value: *Priceless*

ABOUT THE FRONTISPIECE

Selected Pins from Pet's Collection

TOP ARCH *(left to right)*

DOVE WITH OLIVE BRANCH • Yellow gold pin and carved gold mount of a dove with an olive branch, mid-Victorian era. $150.00–250.00.

MOURNING PIN • Yellow gold pin and mount with a crystal covered sepia painting on ivory of a lady in a Grecian dress beside a tomb and a broken anchor, Georgian era. $400.00–700.00.

DOUBLE KNOT • Yellow gold pin and rope mount entwined around a coil of plaited hair, mid-Victorian era. $250.00–350.00.

HORSESHOE • Yellow gold pin and horseshoe mount set with 17 mine-cut diamonds, late Victorian era. $500.00–750.00.

SHELL CAMEO • Yellow gold pin and mount set with a shell cameo of three men's faces and a ram's head, mid-Victorian era. $450.00–650.00.

DOG'S HEAD • Yellow gold pin and mount with a painting on porcelain of a Doberman pinscher, signed on reverse: "J.W. Bailey," late Victorian era. $800.00–1,000.00.

LIZARD • Yellow gold pin and mount shaped like a lizard with 17 emeralds, 31 rose-cut diamonds, and two ruby eyes, mid-Victorian era. $800.00–1,200.00.

LOWER ARCH *(left to right)*

SWAN • Yellow gold pin and mount of a swan with a baroque pearl body, five mine-cut diamonds and a mine-cut ruby eye, late Victorian era. $600.00–900.00.

MOONSTONE • Yellow gold pin and mount with a cone-shaped moonstone and five mine-cut diamonds, late Victorian era. $250.00–350.00.

CABOCHON OPAL • Yellow gold pin and mount with an oval cabochon opal surrounded by 14 mine-cut diamonds, late Victorian era. $700.00–1,000.00.

SQUIRREL • Yellow gold pin with white gold mount of a squirrel, pavé set with Persian turquoise, early Victorian era. $200.00–300.00.

LADY'S PORTRAIT • Yellow gold pin and mount set with a painting on porcelain of a lady, signed on the reverse: "Sarlandie - Limoges," late Victorian era. $300.00–500.00.

WOLF'S HEAD • Yellow gold pin with white gold mount of a wolf's head pavé set with pearls and with two ruby eyes, two gold chain dangles are set with pearls, late Victorian era. $600.00–900.00.

FOUR-LEAF CLOVER • Yellow gold pin and mount set with 36 mine-cut diamonds and five pearls, pin marked: "Wm. Smith & Sons" (Wm. Smith & Sons, Providence, R.I.), circa 1900. $500.00–750.00.

STAR AND CRESCENT • Yellow gold pin with platinum mount, with 15 mine-cut diamonds set in the crescent and five in the star surrounding an emerald, pin is marked: "Tiffany & Co.," circa 1900. $800.00–1,100.00.

JOCKEY'S CAP • Yellow gold pin and mount with 15 mine-cut diamonds and nine mine-cut rubies, late Victorian era. $700.00–1,000.00.

BOTTOM CENTER

BEAU KNOT • Yellow gold pin and mount, set with European-cut diamond in an eight-point star, late Victorian period. $200.00–300.00.

AUTHORS' NOTE

So that we do not mislead the reader, we deem it necessary to preface this book with the following statement: In no way do we claim or aspire to be professional gemologists or expert jewelers. We are simply avid collectors of historic, old tie pins.

It is only through more than 30 years of hands-on experience in amassing a personal collection of more than 2,500 stickpins that we have acquired our knowledge in this truly fascinating hobby we wish to share here with you.

It is hoped the information imparted within these pages will be interesting and perhaps beneficial to those who collect, study, and deal in antique stickpins.

— *Jack and Elynore "Pet" Kerins*

CONTENTS

Introduction 1

Collecting Stickpins 2

Prices and Values 3

Pet's Pins 5

Advertising 6

Agates, Onyx, and Ore 11

Amethysts 15

Armament 17

Art Nouveau 19

Birds 21

Bows and Knots 23

Cameos 25

Carvings 31

Celtic and Native American 33

Coins 35

Coral 37

Crescents and Stars 39

Crowns and Fleur-de-Lis 41

Demons, Dragons, and Reptiles 43

Diamonds 45

Dogs 47

Egyptian 49

Emeralds and Green Stones 51

Events and Organizations 53

Faces 57

Fish and Wildlife 59

Flora 61

Hearts and Hands 63

Horseshoes, Horses, and the Hunt 65

Insects 69

Intaglios 71

Lions and Tigers 73

Memorial and Hair 75

Micromosaics, Mosaics, and Pietra Dura 79

Military, Political, and Religious 81

Moonstones 83

Opals 85

Pearls 87

Portraits and Photographs 91

Quartz 93

Rubies and Garnets 95

Sapphires and Blue Stones 97

Signets 99

Skulls, Teeth, and Talons 101

Topaz, Amber, and Citrine 103

Turquoise and Jade 105

Wishbones and Question Marks 107

Miscellaneous and Recently Acquired 109

Stickpin Holders 117

Cases 118

Clutches 119

Where To Find Antique Stickpins 120

The Author and the Collector 120

INTRODUCTION

It is doubtful anyone knows when the first stickpin was made or who made it. Probably, it originated in England, during the middle of the 18th century when the cravat became a part of a gentleman's attire. Reputedly, some of the early stickpins were worn by that British dandy, George Brian "Beau" Brummell (1778–1840), who held a commanding influence in men's fashions when King George IV was still the young Prince of Wales.

Throughout the following century and a half, in Europe and America, the stickpin was a popular adornment for men's neckwear. It stylishly graced the ascots of both gentlemen and ladies who attended the famous Berkshire races and who followed the hounds while chasing the wily fox. Such pins were also used to fasten scarves of elegant women of social prominence.

When the currently favored fore-in-hand tie came into vogue, the stickpin remained in broad, daily use until the mid-1930s, then it slowly gave way to the trend of wearing tie-clips and eventually, tie-tacks.

In the 1970s, the stickpin did experience a rebirth of popularity. It became quite the fad for women to wear them on lapels of jackets and to enhance their blouses and sweaters. Old pins, hidden away in dresser drawers for over three decades, were retrieved, polished, and displayed once again.

The sudden demand for these antiquated tie-pins created a market for reproductions that rapidly appeared in boutiques and costume jewelry departments. Unfortunately, during this trend, many of the fine old pins were ruined when their owners remodeled them by shortening their stems and welding them together, forming a single cluster, creating a brooch-like pin. Some were even converted into bracelets.

While this trend still continues today to some extent, the fad is not as popular, and the demand for antique stickpins once again has shifted to the serious collectors.

COLLECTING STICKPINS

In the early 1960s, my wife, Pet, inherited five beautiful, old stickpins from my father. They had been stowed away and had not seen the light of day for more than 30 years. Since they were family heirlooms, she began wearing them on her blouses and jackets.

Bringing these antique pieces of jewelry to the forefront once again, lead to her receiving others as gifts from relatives and friends who remembered seeing "something like that" stashed away among their own possessions. Naturally, some were kept for sentimental reasons, but Pet did acquire a few that formed the nucleus of her newly founded hobby.

It was then that she began to look for other sources. Antique shops, old jewelry stores, pawn shops, auctions, flea-markets, garage sales, and estate jewelry counters in department stores all produced their share, and her collection grew.

At first, like many neophyte collectors, Pet pounced on practically every stickpin she found, buying it simply because it was old, and stickpins were difficult to find. Each discovery was heralded triumphantly. She haphazardly became an accumulator rather than a collector.

Then she came to realize that an astounding diversity existed in kinds of stickpins. (More than 50 specific categories are listed in this book.) She also discovered that many of the pins she was finding were duplicates of what she already had, and that some were apparently more common than others. Lovers' knots, crescents, wishbones, horseshoes, and solitary gemstones, for example, were easier to come by than cameos, carvings, or portraits. She also came to recognize variations in materials and quality of workmanship.

Now, a decision had to be made. Was she going to specialize in one, or perhaps just a few, classifications of stickpins? This would narrow the quantity down considerably, but since the pins took up very little space anyway, she opted for a general collection, featuring examples of all the different kinds.

Eventually, Pet became cognizant of the fact that she actually knew next to nothing about the items she was collecting. She needed help, and looked for references. There were none directly related to stickpins. However, she was able to assemble a small library of books on antique jewelry and gem stones.

The publications were worth their weight in gold, and she began to look at her hobby in a different light. Her purchases were now made in a more careful and selective manner. She now recognized mistakes made in the past and endeavored not to repeat them.

Looking back on it now, she deeply regrets those errors, for many of the stickpins she passed up in those days are practically impossible to find today, and the prices of those few that are still available are now much higher by comparison.

She well remembers visiting a small antique shop in the Old Town district of Chicago. This was not long after she began her collection, in the early 1960s. She bought an assortment of ten rather ordinary stickpins, but passed on the purchase of one, even though it was "real nice." After all, who would pay $35.00 for just one pin when they could have ten for the same price – right? Besides, $35.00 was about all she could afford to spend at the time.

That lone stickpin was a small, but beautifully done, portrait of a lady. It was hand painted on porcelain with a gold mounting. The letter accompanying it authenticated its maker as being Peter Fabergé, once jeweler to the Russian czars. Today, a price in four figures would undoubtedly be asked by some of the more prestigious antique jewelry dealers in New York or London.

That was not her only goof, although it topped them all. Another time in the "Windy City," at the estate jewelry counter of Marshall Field & Company, she turned down the asking price of $50.00 for a stickpin. It was a gold mounted painting on porcelain of a dog, and it was signed on the back, "'Wm. B. Ford."

Then there was that time at an antique show, when she chanced upon a stickpin with a coil of hair under glass set in a gold mounting. She refused to buy it because its zig-zag stem was "too badly bent out of shape." The price was next to nothing, and the dealer, who knew no more than Pet, offered to knock off a couple more bucks, suggesting that perhaps the stem could be straightened. Pet realizes now the pin was made that way sometime during the mid-Georgian period, probably around 1780.

In the past 30 years, Pet has become well educated in the many aspects of her collection. The fascination of adding to her array of stickpins is always present, and she feels that sharing what she has learned will be of value to someone else thereby enhancing the pleasures of her own hobby.

If what is presented in these pages will be of assistance to beginners or if it will contribute to the existing knowledge of experienced collectors and dealers, then its writing has been well worth the effort. After all, half the fun in accumulating a collection comes from proudly displaying it for others to see and enjoy.

Throughout the following chapters, we hope to cover each factor in pursuing the hobby of collecting antique stickpins in a such a manner that this book will be a ready and valuable reference on the subject, and will perhaps be of benefit to collectors and antique dealers alike.

PRICES AND VALUES

Deciding whether or not the true value of an antique stickpin is worth the price being asked is somewhat akin to filing your IRS tax return. It isn't much fun, but it's something that regularly presents itself. If you are a serious collector, you will be faced with making evaluations and decisions on a more or less continual basis.

In any sales/purchase transaction, the prime requisites are a seller willing to sell and a buyer willing to buy. It's that gray area in between – the price – that brings on the stress of making up one's mind.

"Is it worth it? Should I spend that much for it?" These are questions you must constantly deal with, and no one else can answer them for you. The conclusion must be reached by you alone. There are, however, several things to consider that may assist you in reaching your ultimate decision.

You must first of all ask yourself if you can afford the price being asked. If the answer is yes, and you definitely want the stickpin for your collection, then its price must be weighed against its value as you determine it.

In making such determinations, the most valuable tool a stickpin collector can own is a good jeweler's loupe, and it should be carried at all times. It is indispensable when appraising the quality, condition, and value of the pin prior to its purchase. It is equally useful at home when cleaning and studying the pieces in your collection. Pet's recommendation is a ten power (10X) loupe.

Your primary inspection of a pin must tell you if it is a genuine antique and not a reproduction. Many repros are easily recognized as outright junk. Some, however, are finely made and desirable pieces but are of current manufacture and should not be evaluated as antiques. You must also be aware that some pins you find may be conversions. In their original state these may not have been stickpins at all, but possibly made up from other pieces of old jewelry such as cuff links or pendants.

Attention should be given to the overall condition of the pin. Are there stones missing? Are there breaks in the metal? Replacements and repairs are often expensive, and matching some of the old stones and metals may be impossible.

The material make-up of the pin should be next on your check list. Is it gold, silver, platinum, brass, or pot-metal? Does it feature precious or semi-precious stones, or are those sparkling things rhinestones, paste, or pop-bottle?

How about workmanship? Beauty in craftsmanship will have a bearing on the value. Some rare pieces are exquisite artwork examples of famous jewelers, and as such, must be valued accordingly. If, for instance, the maker can definitely be identified as Tiffany, or Cartier, or

Fabergé, or Castellani you may have to refinance your home in order to meet the price.

All else being equal, a pin of unique or unusual design will normally be valued slightly higher than one of a motif that was copied in greater numbers.

The rarity and age of a stickpin also governs its price. Pieces from the Georgian era are rare and often found only in museums. If you should come across such a prize, it will usually cost more than one from the Victorian, Art Nouveau, or Art Deco eras.

Historical value is another factor that could govern the price of a stickpin. If, perchance, it can be authenticated as having been owned or worn by some prominent individual or if it was related to some spectacular event, then that fact alone will undoubtedly demand a higher evaluation. Most such items are untouchable and rest only in guarded exhibits, but every now and then, some alert antique hunter will turn up a rare find.

Of course, the old theory of supply and demand will effect the price asked for any item. Since the availability of truly old stickpins is limited to their survival from eras past, and since the number of collectors has been increasing, prices have naturally escalated. In recent years, however, the major influence that pushed up values came with the deregulation of the gold standard, accelerating the appraisals of precious metals. The market value of gold quickly rose from the pegged price of $35.00 to more than $800.00 an ounce.

Not only did the material content of a stickpin increase, but with the overnight jump in the metals market, literally thousands of independent salvage buyers opened small shops advertising: "Now Buying Gold And Silver... Highest Prices Paid For Old Coins & Jewelry." They were interested strictly in the melt-down weight of the metal. People cleaned out drawers and trunks of outdated and no-longer-wanted items and cashed them in for a few ready bucks.

Many antique tea and silverware sets, rings, watches, bracelets, necklaces, and yes, fine old stickpins fell victim. This cut into the supply of the already hard to come-by pins, automatically advancing their prices even more. Eventually, the rapid growth in the metals market peaked and gradually retreated to more sensible and halfway stabilized figures.

All of this did have a lasting effect on the price picture of stickpin collecting. Some of the same pieces we once purchased for $2.00 to $10.00 are today selling for $30.00 to $50.00 and more.

Today, if a serious buyer finds a pin worthy of a place in his or her collection, "the good ol' days" must be forgotten and the present going price reluctantly paid. This brings us to another consideration in deciding whether or not you should purchase that stickpin. That is its desirability.

Here, again, the call is up to you. If you want it badly enough, and if you can afford it, then buy it. More than likely, if you do not, you will continue to stew about it, and as time passes, that stickpin will look better and better.

All of this leaves collectors of antique stickpins in a quandary, for there is little in the way of price guidelines available. Comparison pricing, by visiting antique shops and shows, will certainly help, but even here prices may be extremely variable.

Recently, Pet and I attended a large antique show featuring quality dealers. At five different booths, we found identical stickpins. They were preserved, green beetles in gold mountings and of like quality and condition These pins are old but are quite common. However, the asking prices ranged from $25.00 to $150.00.

At the same show, we found four dealers offering brass advertising stickpins from the Moline Plow Company. They were all in like condition and priced from $15.00 to $90.00.

Such experiences may show that bargains may still be found if you will just shop around, but they establish absolutely nothing in the way of fixing values.

When we first considered writing this book, we talked to many collectors and dealers, asking what they thought were important features such a book should cover. Almost invariably the first thing mentioned was "prices." Setting a level or parity in the pricing of antique jewelry, however, we feel is an impossibility. There are just plain too many variables.

The old adage, "One man's junk is another man's treasure," is one example. Then, the geographical location of a dealer and his clientele is another. The asking price of a stickpin at an antique show in the rural Midwest, for instance, could possibly he multiplied as much as five times when offered for sale in New York City or London.

Fluctuating economic conditions, exorbitant prices being paid by foreign buyers, fads, fashions, wars, natural disasters, and who knows what else can all have a bearing on the buying and selling markets that govern the price of any given item, including antique stickpins.

About all we can offer here are strictly "ballpark" figures gleaned from our current observations and experiences while seeking additions to Pet's collection.

PET'S PINS

In presenting this collection of antique stickpins, we have listed them alphabetically by category together with their descriptions in relation to their location on the color plates. Because of specific designs, some pins will overlap into other categories. Pearls, for example, are listed in their own section; a horseshoe, set with pearls, may be found with pins in the category entitled "Horseshoes, Horses, and the Hunt." We have attempted to give as much information possible about individual pins, including materials, makers, markings, circa, and approximate values at the time of this writing. Where the exact dates of manufacture are unknown, we have used the commonly accepted historical periods to cover the pin's era of production:

> THE GEORGIAN ERA (1714 through 1830)
> In England, this would be the era ruled by the four Kings, George I, II, III, and IV. In America, it would cover Colonial times, through the Revolution, and the beginning of the Westward Movement.

> THE VICTORIAN ERA (1837 through 1901)
> In England, this would cover the reign of Queen Victoria. In America, it would extend from the Westward Movement, through the California Gold Rush, and the Civil War.

> THE ART NOUVEAU ERA (1890 through 1918)
> In England, this would cover most of the Late Victorian Period, on through the Edwardian Period (1901-1910), and World War I.

> THE ART DECO ERA (1920 through 1935)
> In America, it covers the Roaring Twenties, the era of the Great Depression. For all practical purposes, this will bring us to the end of the antique stickpin era and to the collectors of today.

ADVERTISING

U.S. MAIL • *Gold-filled pin and mount shaped in the likeness of a postal worker driving a four wheel mail delivery wagon drawn by two horses; wagon is marked in raised letters: "RURAL FREE DEL'Y" and "U.S. MAIL ROUTE." The roadbed beneath the wagon is marked: "R.F.D. U.S.A.," late Victorian era.* $40.00–50.00.

Advertising stickpins per se are generally of little value in material content. Most were made as cheaply as possible, for they were give-away items. They are currently popular, collectible pieces, and their values have increased dramatically in recent years. Certain examples are very scarce and may sell for $100.00 or more.

While they were usually made in great numbers, in order to disseminate the name of the company or product, they were for the most part considered valueless. Once their novelty waned, they were often thrown away. Large numbers vanished over the years as did many of the trade names they represented.

Examples that have survived are indeed collectible today, and they do represent a piece of the commercial and industrial history of bygone years.

PLATE 1

FIRST ROW *(left to right)*

TOOL COMPANY • Silver plate on copper pin and mount with company logo on front and lettered "Bishop's Saws" on the reverse. The pin maker's name "Greenduck Co., Chi" also appears on the reverse, Art Deco era. $20.00–30.00.

PAINT COMPANY • Silver plate on copper pin and company logo mount of a Chinese man with a paintbrush lettered "CHINAMEL," Art Deco era. $20.00–30.00.

BICYCLE COMPANY • Brass pin with thin metal stamping of company logo reading "NATIONAL CYCLES LEAD," Art Deco era. $20.00–30.00.

SHOE COMPANY • Silver pin and company logo mount of a man in full-dress evening clothes straddling a high top shoe, no company name appears, but pin is stamped "Sterling," Art Deco era. $20.00–30.00.

INSURANCE COMPANY • Silver pin and company logo mount of an elk in a shield and lettered "HARTFORD LIFE INSURANCE CO. Hartford, Conn. Agent's Honor League," reverse is engraved "2nd Degree," pin maker's name "FORBES" and the word "Sterling" are also stamped on reverse, Art Deco era. $25.00–35.00.

SECOND ROW *(left to right)*

SCALE COMPANY • Silver-plated pin and company logo mount of a storekeeper's scales lettered "TOLEDO - NO SPRINGS," Art Deco era. $20.00–30.00.

NATIONAL CASH REGISTER COMPANY • Brass pin and stamped out mount of the company's logo, reverse lettered with pin maker's name "The Whitehead & Hoag Co. Newark, N.J.," circa 1922. $20.00–35.00.

STEAMSHIP COMPANY • Brass pin and enameled logo of an ocean liner marked "KUNGSHOLM," reverse is marked "Lagerstroms Mjolby," Art Deco era. $25.00–35.00.

PAINT COMPANY • Brass pin and mount of company logo, reverse marked "PATTON PAINT CO. Milwaukee," Art Deco era. $15.00–25.00.

TOOL COMPANY • Brass pin and blue and white enameled mount of a circular saw blade company logo lettered "ATKINS ALWAYS AHEAD" and "AAA Trade Mark," Art Deco era. $15.00–25.00.

THIRD ROW *(left to right)*

NEWSPAPER COMPANY • Brass pin and company logo mount of a printing press marked "GR Co," reverse marked "THE GLOBE REGISTER CO. Cincinnati, Ohio," Art Deco era. $20.00–35.00.

TAILORING COMPANY • Brass pin and company logo mount marked "DIXIE TAILORING CO.," pin maker's stamping on reverse "THE GREENDUCK CO. Chicago," Art Deco era. $15.00–25.00.

SEAFOOD COMPANY • Brass pin and thin metal stamping of a fish-shaped company logo lettered "GORTON'S FISH FOODS," Art Deco era. $30.00–40.00.

HORSESHOE COMPANY • Silver-plated pin and company logo mount marked on reverse "UNITED STATES HORSESHOE COMPANY Erie, Pa.," Art Deco era. $20.00–30.00.

FARM EQUIPMENT COMPANY • Brass pin and thin metal stamping of company logo "IHC" (International Harvester Company), pin maker's stamp on reverse "Childs - Chicago," Art Deco era. $25.00–35.00.

FOURTH ROW *(left to right)*

TAILORING COMPANY • Brass pin mounted with transfer of lady's face, reverse marked "NEW YORK INTERNATIONAL COMPANY-TAILORING-CHICAGO," Art Deco era. $20.00– 30.00.

TOOL COMPANY • Brass pin and mount of company's logo shaped like a pair of clippers and marked "BROWN & SHARPE," Art Deco era. $20.00–30.00.

WAGON COMPANY • Brass pin and thin metal stamping of company logo shaped like a wagon wheel crossed by a running greyhound, logo marked "MOLINE WAGON CO. - MOLINE - LIGHT RUNNING AND DURABLE," pin maker's stamp on reverse "S.D. Childs & Co. Chicago," Art Nouveau era. $25.00–35.00.

RAILROAD COMPANY • Brass pin and mount of a uniform button bearing company logo marked "GT" in a circle and "GRAND TRUNK R.R." reverse marked "THOMAS CARLYLE - ASTON - BIRMINGHAM ENGLAND," Art Deco era. $30.00–40.00.

BOTTLING COMPANY • Brass pin mounted with a transfer of a lady's face, reverse marked "WHITE SULPHUR SPRINGS CO. DAVENPORT, IOWA," Art Deco era. $20.00–30.00.

FIFTH ROW *(left to right)*

HOSIERY COMPANY • Brass pin and mount of company logo marked on reverse "PONY STOCKINGS FOR BOYS AND GIRLS," Art Deco era. $15.00–25.00.

NATIONAL CASH REGISTER COMPANY • Brass pin and mount of company's logo, pin maker's stamping on reverse "Greenduck Co. Chicago," Art Deco era. $25.00–35.00.

CANDY COMPANY • Brass pin mounted with a transfer of a lady's face, reverse is marked "MILADY CHOCOLATES," Art Deco era. $20.00–30.00.

EQUIPMENT COMPANY • Gold filled on brass pin and mount of company logo of a hand holding a plow blade, logo marked "J.I. CASE PLOW WORKS RACINE, WIS.," Art Deco era. $40.00–50.00.

TRANSPORTATION COMPANY • Brass pin and mount of a company's logo showing a trolley car and marked "W.E.E.," Art Deco era. $20.00–30.00.

SIXTH ROW *(left to right)*

EQUIPMENT COMPANY • Brass pin and mount of a company logo shaped like a hand plow and marked "P. & O. CANTON," Art Deco era. $30.00–40.00.

PLATE 1

EQUIPMENT COMPANY • Brass pin and thin stamped metal mount of the JOHN DEERE COMPANY logo of a running deer and a hand plow, Art Deco era. $30.00–40.00.

TOOL COMPANY • Brass pin and mount of a company logo shaped like a micrometer and marked "B. & S. MFG. CO. PROV., R.I.," (Bennett & Sawyer Co.), circa 1915. $20.00–30.00.

SHOWN AT BOTTOM

TOOL COMPANY • Brass pin and mount of company logo shaped like a hammer and marked on handle "HAMMER DRY PLATE CO.," Art Deco era. $15.00–25.00.

PLATE 2

FIRST ROW (left to right)

ROUND OAK STOVE COMPANY • Brass pin and mount of an Indian's head marked "DOE-WAH-JACK," reverse marked "ROUND OAK STOVES, RANGES, FURNACES," and stamped with pin maker's name "F. H. Nobel, Chicago," circa 1900. $25.00–35.00.

ROUND OAK STOVE COMPANY • Brass pin and mount of an Indian's head marked "DOE-WAH-JACK," reverse marked "FROM ROUND OAK FOLKS," and stamped with pin maker's name "F.H. Nobel, Chicago," circa 1900. $25.00–35.00.

ROUND OAK STOVE COMPANY • Brass pin and two-sided mount with an Indian's head on the pommel of a sword, the guard marked on one side "DOE-WAH-JACK" and on the other "ROUND OAK," circa 1900. $25.00–35.00.

ROUND OAK STOVE COMPANY • Brass pin and mount shaped like an old-fashioned heating stove marked "ROUND OAK - DOWAGIAC" and stamped with founder's name "P.D. BECKWITH," circa 1900. $40.00–50.00.

ROUND OAK STOVE COMPANY • Brass pin and mount in the shape of a Dutch boy holding a sign marked "ROUND OAK STOVES," reverse marked "Est. P.D. BECKWITH, DOWAGIAC," circa 1900. $25.00–35.00.

ROUND OAK STOVE COMPANY • Brass pin and oval mount with head of an Indian and marked "DOE-WAH-JACK," reverse marked "ROUND OAK STOVES FURNACES - BECKWITH" and with pin maker's name "S.D. CHILDS, CHICAGO," circa 1900. $25.00–35.00.

ROUND OAK STOVE COMPANY • Brass pin and mount of Indian's head marked "DOE-WAH-JACK," reverse marked "ROUND OAK STOVES-RANGES-FURNACES" and marked with pin maker's name "F.H. Nobel, Chicago," circa 1900. $25.00–35.00.

SECOND ROW (left to right)

COFFEE COMPANY • Silver-plated pin and mount of company's logo, a great horned owl, reverse marked "OWL BRAND COFFEES," Art Deco era. $15.00–25.00.

CEMENT COMPANY • Silver plate on copper coin and mount of company's logo, Annie Oakley, with a reverse marked "LEHIGH PORTLAND CEMENT CO. INDIANAPOLIS, IND.," Art Deco era. $15.00–25.00.

CC CO. • Brass pin and gold-plated mount of a spatula superimposed on a clear enameled oval, reverse lettered "C C Co. SPATULA CLUB," Art Deco era. $10.00–20.00.

STOVE COMPANY • Brass pin and mount of company's logo marked "PEORIA STOVES Manufactured by CULTER & PROCTOR STOVE CO. Peoria, Ill.," reverse marked with pin maker's name "The Whitehead & Hoag Co. Newark, N.J.," circa 1922. $15.00–25.00.

ELECTRIC COMPANY • Brass pin and mount shaped like a light bulb and superimposed with the image of Louis XV of France, the patron saint of St. Louis, Missouri. Bulb is lettered "ST. LOUIS ELECTRICAL SHOW 1910," reverse lettered with company name "BASTIAN BROS. CO. ROCH. N.Y.," circa 1910. $15.00–25.00.

INSURANCE COMPANY • Brass pin and oval mount superimposed with image of a coal burning railroad engine, reversed marked "THE TRAVELERS INSURANCE CO. HARTFORD, CONN. TICKET DEPARTMENT," Art Deco era. $35.00–45.00.

COFFEE COMPANY • Silver-plated pin and mount shaped like a square coffee can and marked "STATUE BLEND HIGHGRADE COFFEE" with an illegible signature, Art Deco era. $15.00–25.00.

THIRD ROW (left to right)

COCA-COLA COMPANY • Brass pin and mount shaped like a Coke glass and marked with the company logo in script, Art Deco era. $15.00–25.00.

EQUIPMENT COMPANY • Brass pin and mount shaped like a bare foot and marked "EMERSON BRANTINGHAM CO. FOOT LIFT FARM IMPLEMENTS ROCKFORD, ILL.," Art Deco era. $25.00–35.00.

TEA COMPANY • Brass pin and company logo mount shaped like a tea leaf and marked on the reverse "LIPTON'S TEAS," Art Deco era. $10.00–20.00.

STOVE COMPANY • Gold-plated pin and disc-shaped mount with an Indian's head marked "DOE-WAH-JACK" and "ROUND OAK STOVES RANGES FURNACES," reverse marked "ESTATE OF P.D. BECKWITH DOWAGIAC, MICHIGAN" and pin maker's identification marks "No. 8 E & Co., Chicago," circa 1900. $25.00–35.00.

SHOE COMPANY • Brass pin and company logo mount shaped like a dancing Indian and marked "THE GOTZIAN SHOE," Art Deco era. $20.00–30.00.

EQUIPMENT COMPANY • Brass pin and mount of company's logo shaped like an eagle sitting atop a world globe and lettered "J.I. CASE THRASHING MACHINE CO. INCORPORATED RACINE, WIS. U.S.A.," Art Deco era. $25.00–35.00.

BOTTLING COMPANY • Gold-plated pin and mount of company's logo shaped like a Coke bottle and marked "COCA-COLA," Art Deco era. $15.00–25.00.

FOURTH ROW (left to right)

HAIR GROOMING COMPANY • Gold-filled pin and mount of company's logo with blue inlaid enameled background reading "CLAIROL" and set with a 2mm mine-cut ruby, reverse marked "1/20 G.F.," Art Deco era. (Note: This pin was probably given as a sales or retirement award.) $35.00–50.00.

FOOD COMPANY • Brass pin and inlaid enameled oval of company's logo showing a Dutch boy and girl holding food trays, reverse marked "THE VAN CAMP PACKING CO. INDIANAPOLIS, IND.," Art Deco era. $20.00–30.00.

CLEANSER COMPANY • Brass pin with blue and white inlaid enameled company logo of a running Dutch woman holding a rolling pin, reverse marked "OLD DUTCH CLEANSER CHASES DIRT," Art Deco era. $25.00–35.00.

INSURANCE COMPANY • Gold-filled pin and locket mount with company's logo of American Victory, inside of locket engraved "NATIONAL OF HARTFORD," Art Deco era. $45.00–55.00.

EQUIPMENT COMPANY • Brass pin and red inlaid enameled mount shaped like a cream separator marked with company's logo "SHARPLES," Art Deco era. $40.00–50.00.

DAIRY COMPANY • Brass pin blue and white inlaid enameled company logo of a Dutch boy kissing a Dutch girl and the words "TRY IT," girl's milk pail is lettered "Est. 1869," reverse is marked "LINN'S HOLLAND CREAMERY BUTTER CHICAGO," the pin's manufacturer marked "Childs Chicago," Edwardian era. $15.00–25.00.

PLATE 2

PHARMACEUTICAL COMPANY • Gold-filled pin and mount with red and white inlaid enameled company logo shaped like an mortar and pestle bearing the initials "NR" (Nature's Remedy), reversed marked "WARRANTED 20 YEARS," pin maker marked "Robbins Attleboro," Art Deco era. $25.00–35.00.

FIFTH ROW *(left to right)*

SPORTING GOODS COMPANY • Brass pin and mount of company's logo of hunting dog atop and diamond-shaped sign lettered "D&M. Trade Mark," reverse marked "SPORTING GOODS," Art Deco era. $15.00–25.00.

RAILROAD • Brass pin and silver mount of company's logo "C E" (Central Electric), reverse marked "MARCH," Art Deco era. $25.00–30.00.

COOKWARE COMPANY • Yellow gold pin and mount of company's logo marked "COLUMBIAN GHC" (General Housewares Corporation) and set with two 3mm brilliant cut diamonds and an

emerald, reverse marked "T 10K," Art Deco era. (Note: While included in the advertising category, this pin was probably given as a sales or retirement award.) $100.00–150.00.

WATCHMAKER COMPANY • Brass pin and mount of company's logo shaped like a pocket watch and marked "HAMPDEN DUEBER WATCHES Canton Ohio," Art Deco era. $10.00–20.00.

TOOL COMPANY • Brass pin and mount of company's logo shaped like a circular saw blade and a handsaw and marked with red inlaid enameled letters "AAA" (Atkins Always Ahead), reverse marked "ATKINS SILVER STEEL SAWS," pin maker "H.E. Greenduck Co. Chicago," Art Deco era. $10.00–20.00.

RECORDING COMPANY • Brass pin and mount of company's logo shaped like music notes and marked "COLUMBIA RECORDS," Art Deco era. $20.00–30.00.

PIANO COMPANY • Brass pin and mount shaped like an upright player piano, reverse marked "BALDWIN CINCINNATI USA," Art Deco era. $20.00–30.00.

AGATES, ONYX, AND ORE

This category covers a broad variety of stones and raw metals in a myriad of eye appealing colors and markings that have attracted the attention and graced the jewelry of people of all lands from the earliest times. We have included here everything from moss agates, tigereyes, and banded onyx, to gold, silver, pyrite, and iron ore.

During the heyday of stickpins each was used in creating fascinating pieces. One of the most entrancing of these materials is the moss agate that does not really contain fossilized moss, as often believed, but crystals of manganese oxide.

Other popular stickpins of the time were set with gold nuggets from the mines of California and Alaska and pieces of grape ore from the iron mines of Minnesota. The pins shown here are among those commonly found by collectors today.

CONGLOMERATE • *Gold-plated pin and round mount set with man-made conglomerate of copper, goldstone, pyrite, iron, and quartz, probably Art Deco era. $20.00–35.00.*

PLATE 3

UPPER ARCH (*left to right*)

AGATE • Silver pin and embossed mount holding an opaque, blue/gray oval cabochon, Art Nouveau era. $30.00–50.00.

AGATE • Gold-filled pin and mount with a translucent, milky colored oval cabochon with reddish-brown markings, Edwardian era. $25.00–40.00.

AGATE • Gold-filled pin and mount with an opaque brown and gray mottled cabochon stone, Edwardian era. $25.00–40.00.

AGATE • 14K gold pin and mount holding a large round red and gray translucent cabochon, Edwardian era. $25.00–40.00.

AGATE • 10K gold pin and mount with a translucent, milky colored oval cabochon with waves of reddish-brown, Edwardian era. $30.00–50.00.

AGATE • Gold-plated pin and silver mount with an opaque, brown and gray oval cabochon lace agate, Edwardian era $25.00–40.00.

FOSSIL • 14K gold pin and mount with an oval cabochon Petoskey stone surrounded by 21 baroque seed pearls, Edwardian era. $60.00–85.00.

SHOWN AT LEFT AND RIGHT SIDES

ONYX • Gold-plated pin and mount with an oval cabochon, white and brown-banded stone, Edwardian era. $20.00–30.00.

FOSSIL • Gold-plated pin and mount with an oval cabochon Petoskey stone, Edwardian era. $20.00–30.00.

MIDDLE ARCH (*left to right*)

MOSS AGATE • 10K yellow gold pin and mount with an oval cabochon with green "moss," late Victorian era. $30.00–50.00.

MOSS AGATE • 10K yellow gold pin and mount with a rectangular stone showing brown "moss," late Victorian era. $35.00–50.00.

MOSS AGATE • 14K yellow gold pin and mount with an oval cabochon and black "moss," late Victorian era. $35.00–60.00.

AGATE • 10K yellow gold pin and mount with a long oval translucent cabochon with brown bands, late Victorian era. $25.00–40.00.

MOSS AGATE • 14K yellow gold pin and mount with a rectangular stone showing brown "moss," late Victorian era. $35.00–55.00.

MOSS AGATE • 10K yellow gold pin and mount with a diamond shaped stone with brown "moss," late Victorian era. $30.00–50.00.

MOSS AGATE • 10K yellow gold pin and mount with a round cabochon stone with brown "moss," late Victorian era. $30.00–50.00.

PLATE 3

LOWER ARCH *(left to right)*

MOSS AGATE • 10K yellow gold pin and mount with long oval opaque cabochon with black "moss," late Victorian era. $30.00–50.00.

ONYX • 14K yellow gold pin and mount with a large cabochon of red and white-banded onyx, late Victorian era. $40.00–60.00.

MOSS AGATE • Gold-filled pin and mount with a long oval cabochon stone with green "moss," late Victorian era. $25.00–40.00.

PLATE 4

UPPER ARCH *(left to right)*

AGATE • 14K yellow gold pin and mount with a teardrop-shaped piece of agate surrounded by 18 Alaskan gold nuggets, reverse of mount is marked "NUGGETS - NATIVE GOLD," circa 1909. $75.00–150.00.

JET • Yellow gold pin and basket mount set with a rough piece of jet, late Victorian era. $25.00–35.00.

GOLD NUGGET • Yellow gold pin with milky quartz laced with gold ore, late Victorian era. $100.00–150.00.

IRON • 14K yellow gold pin and basket mount holding a piece of "grape ore" from mines in the Minnesota's Mesabi Range, late Victorian era. $40.00–60.00.

GOLD • 14K yellow gold pin and a gold nugget on granite rock, late Victorian era. $175.00–225.00.

SILVER • Yellow gold pin mounted with a piece of silver ore showing traces of copper and white quartz, Edwardian era. $35.00–50.00.

PYRITE • 14K yellow gold pin and mount holding a square piece of iron pyrite, Edwardian era. $40.00–60.00.

PYRITE • Gold-plated pin with a hollowed jet bead set with iron pyrite, Edwardian era. $25.00–40.00.

IRON • 10K yellow gold pin and basket mount holding a piece of "grape ore" from an iron mine, late Victorian era. $25.00–35.00.

CENTERED UNDER UPPER ARCH

GOLD AND QUARTZ • 10K yellow gold pin and mount holding a piece of white quartz laced with flecks of gold ore, late Victorian era. $35.00–50.00.

SHOWN AT LEFT AND RIGHT

AGATE • Gold-plated pin and mount set with an oval-banded cabochon stone, Edwardian era. $25.00–40.00.

CAT'S EYE • 10K yellow gold pin and hexagon mount with a Greek key design and set with a round, honey-colored cabochon stone, late Victorian era. $30.00–50.00.

SECOND ARCH *(left to right)*

CAT'S EYE • Gold-plated pin and mount with a green, oval cat's eye, late Victorian era. $25.00–40.00.

CAT'S EYE • 10K gold pin and mount with a teardrop-shaped honey-colored cabochon stone, late Victorian era. $35.00–60.00.

TIGEREYE • Gold-filled pin and mount shaped like a human eye and set with a round cabochon tigereye, Art Nouveau era. $30.00–50.00.

CAT'S EYE • Yellow gold pin and mount set with an oval cabochon stone, pin is marked "10K," late Victorian era. $30.00–50.00.

TIGEREYE • Gold-filled pin and mount set with a long oval cabochon stone, late Victorian era. $35.00–50.00.

TIGEREYE • Gold-plated pin and mount set with an oval cabochon stone, late Victorian era. $35.00–45.00.

TIGEREYE • Gold-plated pin and mount set with an oval cabochon stone, late Victorian era. $35.00–45.00.

CAT'S EYE • 14K yellow gold pin and mount set with a round cabochon stone, reverse of mount marked "14K," late Victorian era. $45.00–70.00.

AGATE • Silver pin and mount set with a teardrop-shaped piece of dark green, banded agate, pin has illegible hallmark, Edwardian era. $25.00–40.00.

BOTTOM ARCH *(left to right)*

TIGEREYE • 14K gold pin and clover motif mount set with three round cabochon tigereye stones and a single seed pearl, late Victorian era. $50.00–75.00.

TIGEREYE • Yellow gold pin with rose and white gold mount set with an oval cabochon stone, late Victorian era. $50.00–75.00.

AGATE • Yellow gold pin and mount set with an oval piece of dark brown, banded agate, reverse of mount is marked "10K," late Victorian era. $30.00–50.00.

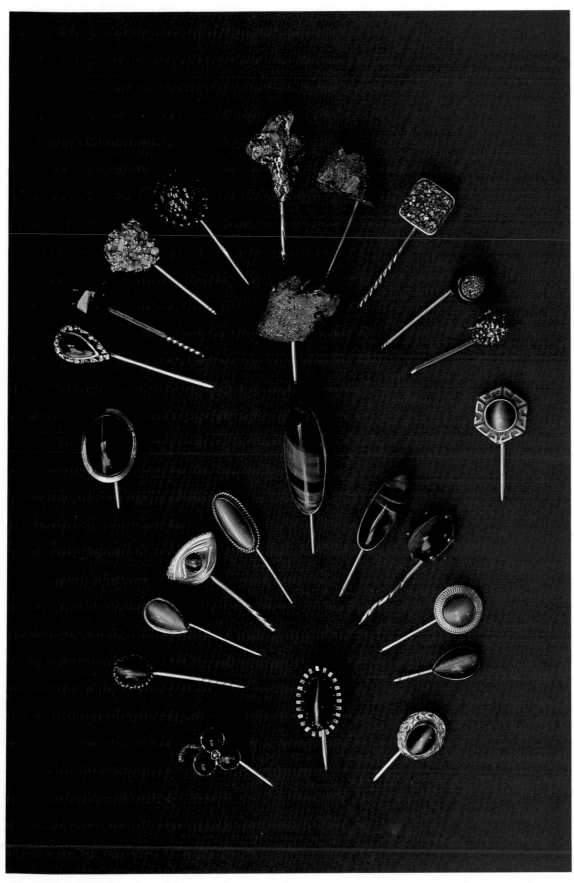

PLATE 4

AMETHYSTS

Commonly accepted as the birthstone of February, the amethyst is a very popular and moderately priced gem of transparent quartz that comes in various shades of purple. Today, it is found and mined in certain areas of South America, the United States, and Canada.

As is true with many gemstones, in ancient times, the amethyst was thought to have mystic powers capable of relieving the afflictions of those who wore them. It was highly treasured by the early Greeks and Romans, where its purple color also associated it with royalty. Later, in England and other areas of Europe, it was widely favored in the jewelry fashions of the Victorian era. Some very beautiful examples of this stone may still be found when viewing the British Crown Jewels.

During the late Georgian era, the amethyst was said to be the favorite gem of Catherine the Great, Empress of Russia.

ROUND AMETHYST • *Yellow gold pin and four pronged gold mount set with a 10mm brilliant cut stone, Art Deco era.* $75.00–100.00.

PLATE 5

UPPER ARCH *(left to right)*

FLORAL MOTIF • Brass pin mounted with molded glass imitation of an amethyst in the shape of a rose, Art Deco era. $5.00–10.00.

ROUND AMETHYST • Yellow gold pin and four pronged gold mount set with a 10mm brilliant cut stone, Art Deco era. $75.00–100.00.

AMETHYST • Yellow gold pin and mount set with a European-cut stone, late Victorian era. $50.00–75.00.

OVAL AMETHYST • Yellow gold pin and mount set with a large stone. Table is incised with a gold floral motif and three tiny rose-cut diamonds, mid-Victorian era. $100.00–125.00.

EMERALD CUT AMETHYST • Gold-plated pin and mount set with a large stone, Edwardian era. $30.00–50.00.

AMETHYST • Gold-plated pin and mount set with a bullet shaped stone framed by 23 faceted crystals, Edwardian era. $40.00–60.00.

AMETHYST • Yellow gold pin and flat embossed round mount set with a European-cut stone, Edwardian era. $50.00–75.00.

OVAL AMETHYST • Yellow gold pin and mount set with a large oval stone, late Victorian era. $85.00–100.00.

AMETHYST • Gold-plated pin and mount set with an oval, dome-cut amethyst and four clear rhinestones, Edwardian era. $10.00–20.00.

SHOWN AT LEFT AND RIGHT

AMETHYST • Yellow gold pin and mount set with a round brilliant cut stone surrounded by four blue inlaid enamel hearts, late Victorian era. $45.00–65.00.

INVERTED TEARDROP AMETHYST • Yellow gold pin and mount set with an amethyst and a baroque pearl, pin is marked "14K," late Victorian era. $75.00–100.00.

CENTER ARCH *(left to right)*

ROUND AMETHYST • Yellow gold pin and mount with the stone encircled by 21 seed pearls, pin is marked "10K," late Victorian era. $65.00–85.00.

ROUND AMETHYST • Yellow gold pin with a sterling silver mount set with a round amethyst and eight mine-cut clear stones, late Victorian era. $75.00–100.00.

ROUND AMETHYST • Yellow gold pin and a gold filigree mount set with stone and a brilliant cut diamond, Edwardian era. $75.00–100.00.

OVAL CABOCHON AMETHYST • Yellow gold pin and mount with a cabochon stone, late Victorian era. $50.00–75.00.

LARGE AMETHYST • Yellow gold pin and mount set with an oval stone carved in relief in the likeness of two swans, pin is marked "14K," late Victorian era. $100.00–150.00.

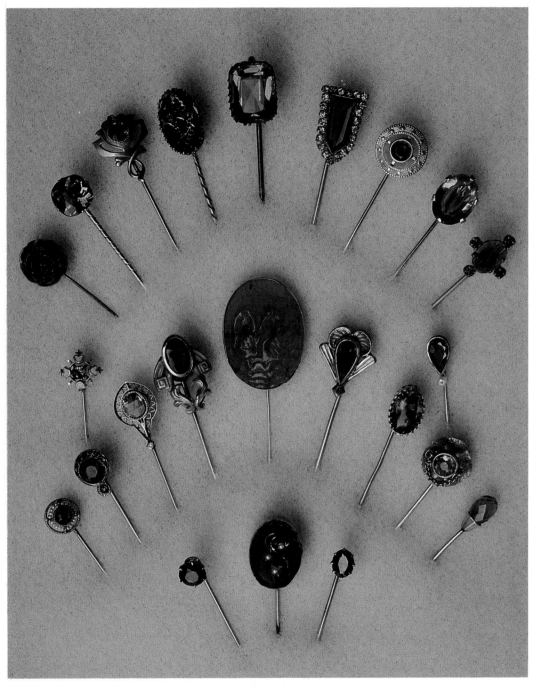

PLATE 5

INVERTED TEARDROP AMETHYST • Yellow gold pin and mount with a pear-shaped stone, Edwardian era. $50.00–75.00.

OVAL CABOCHON AMETHYST • Yellow gold pin and basket mount with a cabochon stone, pin is marked with illegible benchmark, late Victorian era. $60.00–85.00.

ROUND AMETHYST • Yellow gold pin and hammered gold mount trimmed with a gold chain set with a brilliant cut stone, pin is marked "14K," Edwardian era. $75.00–100.00.

AMETHYST SCARF PIN • Yellow gold pin and mount set with a fully faceted briolette-cut stone, Edwardian era. $50.00–75.00.

BOTTOM ARCH (*left to right*)

ROUND AMETHYST • Yellow gold pin and Tiffany type mount set with a brilliant cut stone, pin is marked "10K," Edwardian era. $35.00–50.00.

OVAL AMETHYST • Gold-plated pin and mount set with a flat surfaced stone that is incised in gold and set with three seed pearls, mid-Victorian era. $50.00–75.00.

OVAL AMETHYST • 10K yellow gold pin and Tiffany type mount set with an oval-cut stone, Edwardian era. $75.00–100.00.

ARMAMENT

From his early beginning, man has armed himself with weapons for reasons of self-preservation and the defense of what was his, or at times, to take from his fellow man that which was not. Down through centuries, the evolution of weapons has seen many changes, from the rocks and clubs of cave dwelling Neanderthal's to the nuclear tools of destruction in our, so called, civilized world of today.

In that somewhere in between came the era of the stickpin, and it seems only natural that the weapons motif would be a popular theme of its time.

Since the sword has been the most representative item of weaponry, it only stands that the noble blade should hold a dominating influence in the motifs of stickpins that graced gentlemen's fashions of the times.

CAVALIER • *Yellow gold pin with a pedestal-shaped silver mount holding a silver, highly detailed, fully three-dimensional likeness of a cavalier with a gold sword in hand, gold accents on his clothing from the epaulets on his shoulders down to the buckles on his shoes, late Victorian era.* $400.00–500.00.

PLATE 6

UPPER ARCH *(left to right)*

RAPIER • Silver filigree, probably made in Italy, late Victorian era. $20.00–40.00.

DRESS SABER • Yellow gold of Prussian cavalry type with blue enameled guard set with four seed pearls, the scabbard is attached with gold chain, late Victorian era. $75.00–100.00.

WARRIOR'S FACE • Gold-plated pin with blackened brass right profile of a Spanish conquistador with gold-plated helmet and breast plate, Edwardian era. $45.00–75.00.

HELMET AND SWORD • Yellow gold pin with three-dimensional, French style helmet complete with chin strap and sword in yellow gold inlaid with blue and white enamel, late Victorian era. $400.00–500.00.

WARRIOR'S FACE • Gold-plated pin with blackened brass left profile of a Spanish conquistador with gold-plated helmet and epaulets, Edwardian era. $45.00–75.00.

DRESS SWORD • Yellow gold French style set with 19 graduated pearls in hilt and guard, gold scabbard with pearl at tip is attached with a gold chain, late Victorian era. $75.00–100.00.

RAPIER • Yellow gold with a disc of abalone set in hand guard, Edwardian era. $15.00–30.00.

SHOWN AT LEFT AND RIGHT

DRESS DIRK • Yellow gold hilt set with two seed pearls and a tiny mine-cut ruby, late Victorian era. $45.00–60.00.

DIRK AND WREATH • Silver, probably World War I memorial pin, circa 1918. $15.00–25.00.

CENTER ARCH *(left to right)*

RAPIER • Yellow gold wire with three tiny rhinestones and three tiny amethysts set in guard, stones are mine-cut, late Victorian era. $40.00–60.00.

DRESS SWORD • Yellow gold with white and blue inlaid enameled grip, late Victorian era. $35.00–50.00.

DRESS SWORD • Yellow gold with white enameled grip and four small pearls set in hilt, late Victorian era. $40.00–60.00.

DRESS SWORD • Yellow gold with mother-of-pearl grip and two seed pearls set in hilt, late Victorian era. $25.00–45.00.

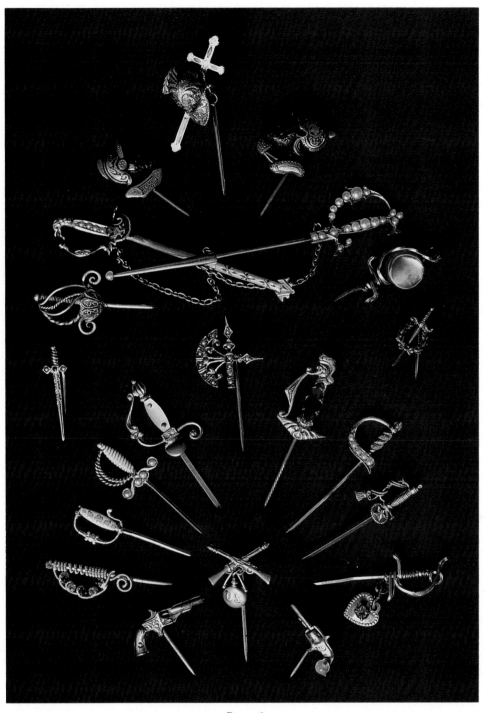

PLATE 6

BATTLE AX • Yellow gold set with 13 seed pearls, late Victorian era. $65.00–85.00.

DRESS SWORD • Gold-plated with red glass set in grip, Edwardian era. $5.00–15.00.

DRESS SWORD • Yellow gold with five seed pearls set in guard, reverse side of blade is marked "14K," late Victorian era. $50.00–65.00.

CIVIL WAR OFFICER'S DRESS SWORD • Yellow gold blade and hilt with raised star and white gold wrapped grip with yellow gold cord and tassel, reverse of blade marked "14K," late Victorian era. $65.00–85.00.

DRESS SWORD • Yellow gold with gold heart dangle set with tiny mine-cut clear stone, late Victorian era. $20.00–35.00.

BOTTOM ARCH *(left to right)*

REVOLVER • White metal pin and three-dimensional gun, Edwardian era. $10.00–20.00.

CROSSED MILITARY RIFLES • Silver with canteen dangle marked on front "U.S.," circa 1918. $25.00–35.00.

REVOLVER • Brass pin and gun with white glass bead set on grip, Edwardian era. $5.00–10.00.

ART NOUVEAU

The Art Nouveau era had its beginning about 1890, in the time of change and transition leading into the turn of the century, and its popularity continued until the beginning of the "Roaring Twenties." Much of the art form exhibited during this period was characterized by swirling shapes, sweeping curves, and wind-blown images. Motifs were dominated by such subjects as flowers and flying birds and especially by the faces and figures of long-haired females.

The era leaned toward a fascination with things natural, iridescent, and irregular. Pearls, especially baroque pearls, opals, and moonstones were very popular as was tortoise shell.

Historically, this new age saw what was probably the peak in the popularity of stickpins.

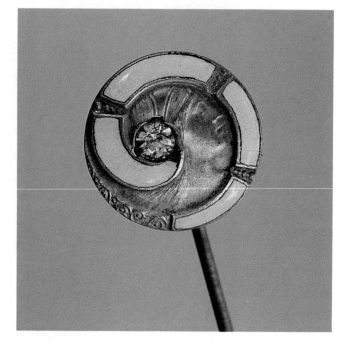

FEMININE FACE • *Yellow gold pin and disc-shaped mount showing the right profile of a lady with flowing hair and set with a 2½mm mine-cut diamond all framed in a white inlaid enameled sweeping curl, reverse of mount is marked "PAT. PEND.," Art Nouveau era. $75.00–100.00.*

PLATE 7

FIRST ROW *(left to right)*

CHERUB • Yellow gold pin and mount shaped in the face of an angel framed by its wings and set with a cabochon ruby, Art Nouveau era. $50.00–60.00.

CHERUB • Yellow gold pin and mount shaped in the winged figure of an angel in right profile playing a flute, Art Nouveau era. $50.00–60.00.

THOR • Sterling silver pin and mount shaped in the right profile face of the Norse god of thunder with his wind-swept hair set with 11 mine-cut rhinestones, reverse of mount is marked "STER," Art Nouveau era. $40.00–60.00.

GIRL AND BIRD • Yellow gold pin and mount shaped in the left profile of a girl with a peacock on her head and set with a mine-cut rhinestone in her ear, Art Nouveau era. $50.00–60.00.

GIRL'S FACE • Gold-plated pin and mount shaped like a long-haired girl's face against the background of a purple enameled flower, pin is marked "H A & CO" (Horton, Angel & Attleboro, Mass.), circa 1916. $30.00–50.00.

SECOND ROW *(left to right)*

GIRL'S FACE • Gold-plated pin and mount shaped like a girl's face in an ornamental frame set with two mine-cut rubies, pin is marked "H A & CO" (Horton, Angel & Co., Attleboro, Mass.), circa 1916. $30.00–50.00.

GIRL'S FACE • Gold-plated pin and mount shaped in the right profile of a long-haired girl set in an ornamental frame, pin is marked "H A & CO" (Horton, Angel & Co., Attleboro, Mass.), circa 1916. $30.00–40.00.

GIRL'S FACE • Gilded pin and thin metal stamped mount in the front view of a girl's face with up-swept hair, Art Nouveau era. $25.00–40.00.

GIRL'S FACE • Gold-plated pin and mount shaped in the left profile of a long-haired girl wearing a headband set with six mine-cut clear stones, Art Nouveau era. $40.00–55.00.

MYTHOLOGY • Gold-plated pin and mount shaped in the left profile of a young goddess surrounded by her own flowing curls, Art Nouveau era. $30.00–40.00.

THIRD ROW *(left to right)*

CLEOPATRA • White metal pin and brass diamond-shaped mount with the raised right profile of Egypt's notorious queen, Art Nouveau era. $25.00–40.00.

GIRL'S FACE • Gold plate on copper pin and stamped thin metal mount of the left profile of a long-haired girl wearing a headband set with three seed pearls, Art Nouveau era. $30.00–45.00.

GIRL'S FACE • Yellow gold pin and right profile mount of a girl with tinted face and a 2mm mine-cut diamond in her hair, pin is marked "14K," Art Nouveau era. $70.00–90.00.

GIRL'S FACE • Yellow gold pin and left profile mount of a long-haired girl with an enameled face, Art Nouveau era. $50.00–60.00.

GIRL'S FACE • Gold-plated pin and oval-shaped gold plate on copper mount of a girl's left profile framed in her long curls, pin is marked "M M CO." (Mautner Mfg. Co., New York, N.Y.), circa 1927. $30.00–40.00.

PLATE 7

FOURTH ROW *(left to right)*

GIRL AND SHEEP • Yellow gold pin and disc-shaped mount showing the raised right profile of the Greek goddess, Ceres, with a 2mm mine-cut diamond in her hair and facing two sheep, pin is marked "14K," Art Nouveau era. $65.00–90.00.

GIRL'S FACE • Gold-plated pin mounted with the front view of a girl's face between the leaves of a lily that is set with seven seed pearls, Art Nouveau era. $35.00–50.00.

GIRL'S FACE • Yellow gold pin and small disc-shaped mount with the raised right profile of a girl looking at a bird, front of mount is set with a 2mm mine-cut diamond and the pin is marked "14K," Art Nouveau era. $60.00–75.00.

GIBSON GIRL • Gold-plated pin and mount in left profile of a girl in a large hat, pin is marked "H A & CO" (Horton, Angel & Co., Attleboro, Mass.), circa 1916. $30.00–40.00.

FEMALE CHILD • Yellow gold pin and left profile mount of girl's face framed in leaves set with a 2mm mine-cut diamond, pin is marked "14K," Art Nouveau era. $65.00–90.00.

FIFTH ROW *(left to right)*

INDIAN FACE • Silver pin and silver plate on brass right profile mount of an Indian brave's face framed in his own windblown hair set with a 2mm mine-cut amethyst, Art Nouveau era. $20.00–30.00.

PRINCESS • Sterling silver pin and right profile mount of a young princess, pin is marked "STERLING," Art Nouveau era. $25.00–35.00.

GIBSON GIRL • Brass pin and right profile mount of a girl in a large hat and set with a 2mm mine-cut rhinestone, Art Nouveau era. $25.00–40.00.

GIRL'S FACE • Sterling silver pin and left profile mount of a girl whose long tresses are set with four rose-cut garnets, Art Nouveau era. $25.00–40.00.

GIRL AND LILY • Sterling silver pin and left profile bust of a girl in Grecian garb among the lilies, pin is marked "STERLING," Art Nouveau era. $25.00–35.00.

BIRDS

From ancient times humans have been fascinated by the grace and beauty of birds – especially those in flight. It was only natural, therefore, that birds should be included in some of the earliest cave and tomb paintings. They were also one of the more often used design motifs in the age when stickpins were commonly popular. This was especially so in the late Victorian and Art Nouveau eras.

The very nature of the subject lends itself to the use of inlaid enamels, precious stones, and pavé gem settings. Many of the pins of this category will be smaller in size when compared to others, while larger, highly detailed three-dimensional birds are more rare and, on the average, a bit more valuable.

FLYING PHOENIX • *Yellow gold pin and round mount holding a cabochon piece of ivory topped with the gold likeness of a Phoenix, the sacred bird of ancient Egyptians, reverse of mount stamped "MICHAUD," late Victorian era. $75.00–125.00.*

PLATE 8

TOP ARCH (*left to right*)

FLYING SWALLOW • Yellow gold pin and bird set with eight seed pearls, pin marked "14K," late Victorian era. $75.00–125.00.

EAGLE'S HEAD • Yellow gold pin and bird's head with a mine-cut ruby eye and a small pearl in beak, reverse of mount is marked "14K," late Victorian era. $150.00–250.00.

A BRACE OF PHEASANTS • Silver pin and birds, one bird has a small pearl in its beak, Art Nouveau era. $25.00–50.00.

SNIPE • Yellow gold pin and oval mount with enameled bird in relief, late Victorian era. $150.00–225.00.

ENGLISH CRYSTAL MOTIF • Gold-plated pin and mount with reverse intaglio painting of a woodcock on gilded background, late Victorian era. $75.00–100.00.

HERON • Yellow gold pin with full figure of bird on an oval yellow gold mount, Edwardian era. $35.00–75.00.

AMERICAN EAGLE'S HEAD • Yellow gold pin with bird's head enameled on gold, Edwardian era. $150.00–200.00.

SMALL FLYING SWALLOW • Gold-plated pin with yellow gold bird with a ruby eye, and a mine-cut crystal dangling from beak, late Victorian era. $50.00–75.00.

PAIR OF DOVES • Gold-plated pin with the stamped out likeness of birds sitting on a branch, Edwardian era. $20.00–30.00.

SHOWN AT LEFT AND RIGHT SIDES

SMALL FLYING SONG BIRD • Yellow gold pin and bird pavé set with 12 mine-cut diamonds and cabochon ruby eye, pin is marked "10K," Edwardian era. $100.00–150.00.

FLYING SWALLOW • Yellow gold pin and bird with four seed pearls set in wings and a rose-cut ruby in its beak, pin is marked "10K," late Victorian era. $50.00–75.00.

BOTTOM ARCH (*left to right*)

GREAT HORNED OWL • Gold-plated pin and white metal bird perched on a branch, bird is pavé set with rhinestones and has red glass eyes, Art Deco era. $15.00–25.00.

PEACOCK • Yellow gold pin and bird with spread wings encircling a baroque pearl, pin is marked "14K," late Victorian era. $50.00–100.00.

FALCON • Silver pin with three-dimensional bird perched on a branch, Art Nouveau era. $25.00–35.00.

FLYING SWALLOW • Yellow gold pin with rose gold bird surrounded by a gold branch with white gold blossoms, pin is marked "10K," late Victorian era. $50.00–75.00.

EAGLE • Yellow gold pin with large, exquisitely detailed, three-dimensional eagle with wings spread while perched on a tree limb guarding a nest set with a large cabochon amethyst in a yellow gold mount, late Victorian era. $300.00–500.00.

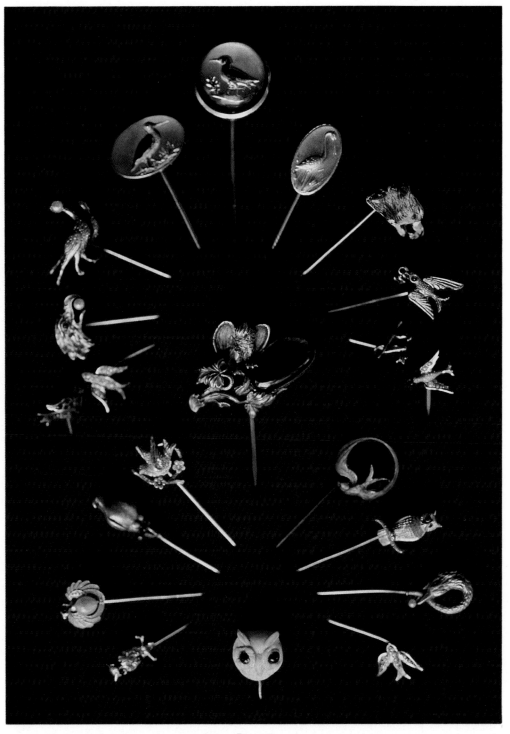

PLATE 8

FLYING SWALLOW • Silver pin and blue enamel on silver bird, pin is bench marked with a crown, old English "T," and a lion, pin is marked "STERLING," British made in the Art Nouveau era. $50.00–75.00.

GREAT HORNED OWL • Yellow gold pin and three-dimensional yellow gold bird perched on a rose gold branch, pin is marked "14K," Edwardian era. $75.00–125.00.

ANHINGA • Yellow gold pin with bird's head and neck in yellow gold with a small pearl in its beak, Art Nouveau era. $45.00–75.00.

SMALL FLYING SWALLOW • Yellow gold pin and bird with eight seed pearls on wings and back, pin is marked "14K," late Victorian era. $75.00–100.00.

CENTERED AT BOTTOM

OWL'S FACE • Gold-plated pin with carved ivory bird's face and glass eyes, Edwardian era. $25.00–50.00.

BOWS AND KNOTS

Motifs symbolizing love, security, and fidelity were often found in many types of antique jewelry. These patterns were extensively used in designing stickpins. Lover's knots (sometimes called beau-knots), entwined rope, and ribbons tied in bows were all in this category.

Bows and knots were considered symbols of binding love and were especially popular during the late Victorian and Edwardian eras. Many of the stickpins of this motif were set with diamonds, rubies, sapphires, and turquoise, for these gems reputedly held magic powers to influence love and fidelity. Both bows and knots are among those most commonly found by collectors today.

Because of their popularity, the craftsmanship and materials exhibited in these pins created an exceptionally wide span in prices and values.

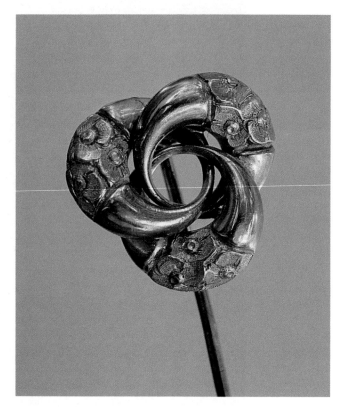

LARGE KNOT • *Rose gold pin and three white and yellow gold interlocking rings with floral engraving, late Victorian era. $50.00–75.00.*

PLATE 9

UPPER ARCH *(left to right)*

LOVER'S KNOT • Yellow gold pin and knot set with a single medium size pearl, pin is marked "14K," Edwardian era. $50.00–75.00.

LOVER'S KNOT • Gold-filled pin and knot set with a large brilliant cut synthetic diamond, pin is marked "1/20 1OK G.F. AMCO," Art Deco period. $35.00–60.00.

LOVER'S KNOT • Yellow gold pin and knot which is engraved and inlaid with enamel and set with a small European-cut diamond, Edwardian era. $50.00–75.00.

LOVER'S KNOT • Yellow gold pin and engraved mount, pin is marked "W & R" (Weigle & Rose Co., Newark, N.J.), circa 1904. $25.00–50.00.

LARGE KNOT • Rose gold pin and three white and yellow gold interlocked rings with floral engravings, Edwardian era. $50.00–75.00.

DOUBLE LOVER'S KNOTS • White gold pin with an engraved white gold knot interlocked with a plain rose gold knot, Edwardian era. $25.00–50.00.

LOVER'S KNOT • Yellow gold pin and knot engraved and inlaid with enamel and set with a small brilliant cut diamond, Edwardian era. $65.00–95.00.

LOVER'S KNOT • Yellow gold pin and engraved knot set with a brilliant cut pink stone, pin is marked "10K," Edwardian era. $40.00–60.00.

BRAIDED ROPE MOTIF • Yellow gold pin and rope motif mount entwined around a Scotch-cut garnet, late Victorian era. $50.00–75.00.

SHOWN AT LEFT AND RIGHT SIDES

BOW • Gold-plated pin and ribbon tied in a bow and set with a single pearl, Edwardian era. $25.00–40.00.

BOW • Gold-plated pin and ribbon tied in a bow and inlaid with white enamel, Edwardian era. $25.00–35.00.

LOWER ARCH *(left to right)*

LOVER'S KNOT • Yellow gold pin and knot set with a 2mm rose-cut garnet, late Victorian era. $30.00–50.00.

LOVER'S KNOT • Yellow gold pin and engraved knot set with a mine-cut diamond, Edwardian era. $50.00–75.00.

KNOT • Gold-filled pin and carved belt twisted into a knot, Edwardian era. $25.00–50.00.

DOUBLE KNOT • Gold-plated pin and plain yellow gold knots set with a small opal, Edwardian era. $35.00–55.00.

DOUBLE KNOT • Yellow gold pin with one plain gold and one engraved gold knot and with a clear mine-cut stone, Edwardian era. $25.00–50.00.

LOVER'S KNOT • Gold-plated pin and knot set with a single garnet, Edwardian era. $25.00–40.00.

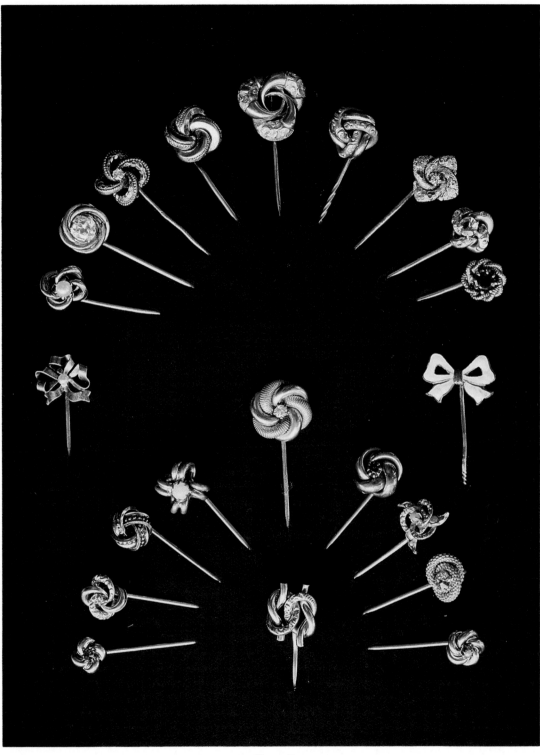

PLATE 9

KNOT AND LEAF MOTIF • Yellow gold pin and knotted vine set with six seed pearls and a turquoise bead, Edwardian era. $40.00–60.00.

LOVER'S KNOT • Yellow gold pin and engraved yellow gold lover's knot set with a 3mm European-cut diamond, Edwardian era. $75.00–125.00.

LOVER'S KNOT • Yellow gold pin and plain yellow gold lover's knot set with a small half pearl, pin is marked "10K," Edwardian era. $35.00–50.00.

CENTERED AT BOTTOM

DOUBLE HALF HITCH • Yellow gold pin with plain and engraved yellow gold knots, late Victorian era. $35.00–50.00.

CAMEOS

Cameos are engravings cut in relief. They are often made of stone or shell composed of two or more layers of different colors so the relief cut will contrast, one layer with another. Agate, sardonyx, and carnelian are among such stones used, but shell, coral, and lava cameos are also common.

Many fine old cameos show exquisite detail and exemplify the rare talents of the artisans who created them. The technique dates as far back as 4000 BC, to the ancient Egyptians, Greeks, and Romans. A revival of the art was seen in the 18th and 19th centuries with beautiful works coming from Italy. Excellent pieces were done in lava from Mt. Vesuvius and coral from the Naples area.

Many of the finest antique stickpins that have survived the years are in the cameo motif.

LADY'S FACE • *Yellow gold pin and mount of a lady's left profile in carved sardonyx, exquisite detail, late Victorian era.* $400.00–600.00.

PLATE 10

UPPER ARCH *(left to right)*

BEARDED MAN • Yellow gold pin and mount, right profile, carved carnelian, late Victorian era. $75.00–150.00.

BEARDED MAN • White gold pin and mount of a man's left profile carved in tigereye, pin is marked "14K," late Victorian era. $75.00–150.00.

LADY'S FACE • Yellow gold pin and mount, high relief, right profile, carved pink coral, mid-Victorian era. $150.00–250.00.

ROMAN MAN'S FACE • Yellow gold pin and mount shown in left profile carved sardonyx, late Victorian era. $150.00–250.00.

LADY'S FACE • Yellow gold pin and mount, very high relief, right profile carved pink coral, late Victorian era. $250.00–400.00.

LADY'S FACE • Yellow gold pin and mount in the left profile of a lady's face carved in shell, early Victorian era. $150.00–250.00.

ANCIENT WARRIOR • Yellow gold pin and mount in the high relief carving in red coral of a warrior's face, pin is marked "14K," mid-Victorian era. $150.00–250.00.

MAN'S FACE • Yellow gold pin and mount of a bearded man's left profile carved in white and black onyx, mid-Victorian era. $100.00–200.00.

LADY'S FACE • White gold pin with white gold filigree mount, of a lady's right profile in high relief carved in shell, pin is marked "14K," late Victorian era. $150.00–250.00.

SHOWN AT LEFT AND RIGHT

LADY'S FACE • Yellow gold pin and teardrop mount of a lady's right profile in a high relief carving in pink coral, mid-Victorian era. $150.00–250.00.

LADY'S FACE • Yellow gold pin and mount of a lady's left profile carved in carnelian, pin is marked "14K," mid-Victorian era. $75.00–150.00.

LOWER ARCH *(left to right)*

LADY'S FACE • Yellow gold pin and mount, right profile, high relief carving in shell, mid-Victorian era. $150.00–250.00.

ANCIENT WARRIOR • Yellow gold pin and mount of a warrior's left profile carved in sardonyx, mid-Victorian era. $275.00–475.00.

LADY'S FACE • Yellow gold pin and mount of a lady's right profile carved in shell, early Victorian era. $150.00–250.00.

LADY'S FACE • Yellow gold pin and mount of a lady's left profile in very high relief carved in lava, mid-Victorian era. $300.00–400.00.

LADY'S FACE • Yellow gold pin and mount of a lady's left profile in exquisitely detailed carved sardonyx, late Victorian era. (Note: This is the same pin used in the category lead photo.) $400.00–600.00.

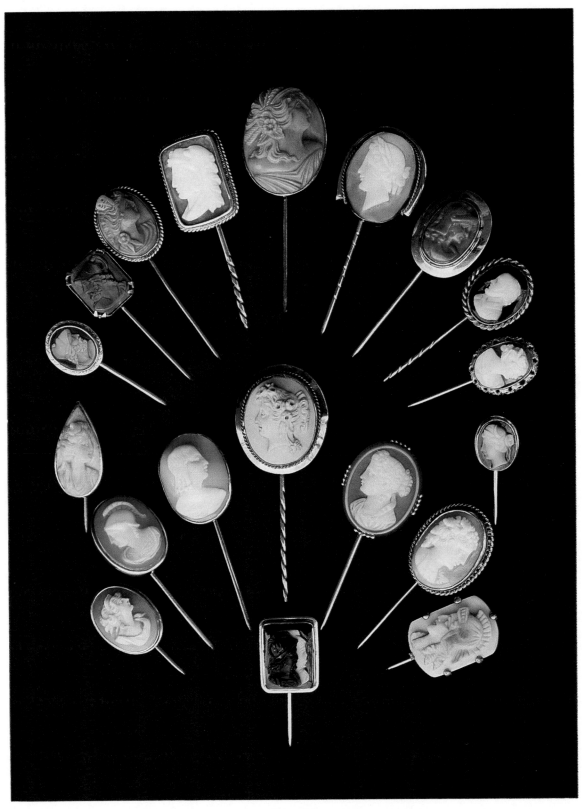

PLATE 10

LADY'S FACE • Yellow gold pin and mount of a lady's right profile carved in shell, pin is marked "10K," mid-Victorian era. $200.00–300.00.

WARRIOR'S FACE • Gold-plated pin and mount in a warrior's left profile carved in shell, mid-Victorian era. $75.00–125.00.

CENTERED AT BOTTOM

VIKINGS • Yellow gold pin and mount, of two Vikings in right profile carved from onyx, Edwardian era. $150.00–250.00.

PLATE 11

UPPER ARCH (*left to right*)

GREEK MUSE • Yellow gold pin and mount, full-figured muse carved in shell, mid-Victorian era. $100.00–175.00.

LADY'S FACE • Yellow gold pin and mount of a lady's right profile carved in white on black onyx, late Victorian era. $75.00–150.00.

MAN'S FACE • Yellow gold double-sided scarf pin and mount of a man's right profile carved in mother-of-pearl and set with moss agate on reverse, pin is marked "14K," mid-Victorian era. $150.00–250.00.

LADY'S FACE • Yellow gold pin and mount of a lady's right profile carved in shell, late Victorian era. $100.00–150.00.

WARRIOR'S FACE • Yellow gold pin and mount of a warrior's right profile carved in sardonyx, late Victorian era. $400.00–600.00.

DOUBLE FACE • Yellow gold pin and mount in high relief left profiles of ancient warriors carved in black on white onyx, late Victorian era. $150.00–250.00.

LADY'S FACE • Yellow gold pin and white gold mount of a lady's left profile carved in moonstone, late Victorian era. $200.00–300.00.

HEAD OF NIKE • Yellow gold pin and mount of the Greek god's left profile carved in moonstone surrounded by four mine-cut diamonds, late Victorian era. $300.00–400.00.

GREEK MUSE • Yellow gold pin and mount in the full-length figure of a muse carved in shell, pin is marked "14K," mid-Victorian era. $100.00–175.00.

SHOWN AT LEFT AND RIGHT

PSYCHE AND CUPID • Yellow gold pin and mount in the full figures of the Greek gods carved in shell, late Victorian era. $100.00–175.00.

REBECCA AT THE WELL • Yellow gold pin and mount in the full figure of Rebecca carved in shell, late Victorian era. $100.00–150.00.

LOWER ARCH (*left to right*)

LADY'S FACE • Yellow gold pin and mount of a lady's right profile in carved shell, pin is marked "10K," late Victorian era. $70.00–150.00.

MAN'S FACE • Yellow gold pin and mount of a man's high relief right profile carved in shell, late Victorian era. $100.00–175.00.

LADY'S FACE • Yellow gold pin and mount of a lady's very high relief right profile carved in lava, late Victorian era. $200.00–300.00.

LADY'S FACE • Yellow gold pin and mount of a lady's very high relief right profile carved in white on black onyx, late Victorian era. $200.00–300.00.

LADY'S FACE • Gold-plated pin and mount of a lady's very high relief left profile carved in shell, late Victorian era. $125.00–175.00.

LADY'S FACE • Yellow gold pin and mount of a lady's right profile carved in white on black onyx, pin is marked "14K," late Victorian era. $100.00–175.00.

GREEK WARRIOR • Yellow gold pin and mount of a warrior's full figure holding spear and shield carved in agate, late Victorian era. $100.00–175.00.

BOTTOM CENTER

LADY'S FACE • Yellow gold pin and mount of a lady's high relief right profile carved in coral, late Victorian era. $75.00–150.00.

LADY'S FACE • Yellow gold pin and mount of a lady's high relief right profile carved in sardonyx, late Victorian era. $175.00–250.00.

SEPTEMBER MORN • Gold-plated pin and mount of a lady bathing in a lake, molded in pink and white glass, late Victorian era. $25.00–50.00.

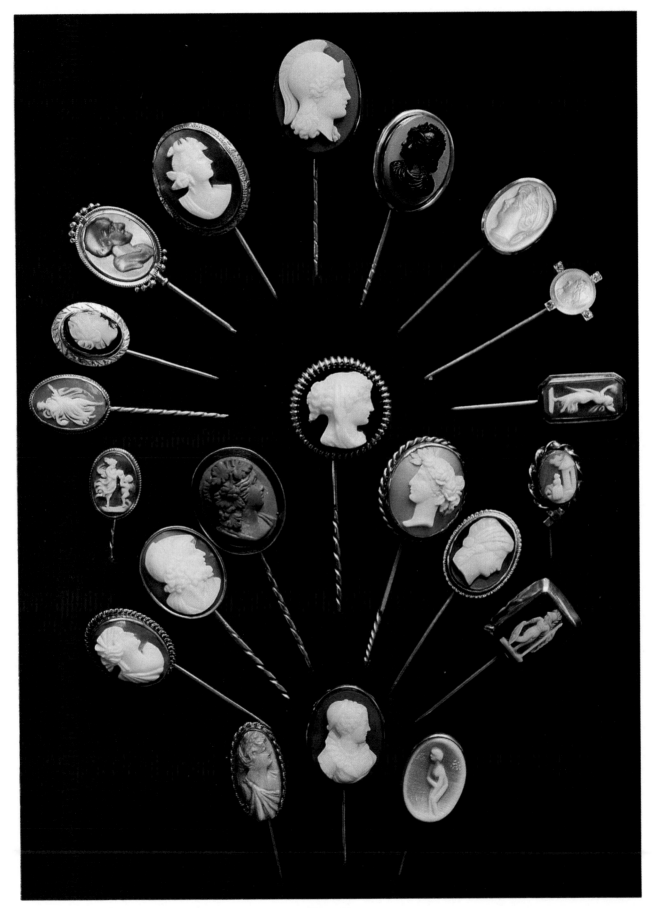

PLATE 11

28

PLATE 12

FIRST ROW *(left to right)*

LADY'S FACE • Yellow gold pin and mount of a lady's right profile carved in white on black onyx, late Victorian era. $75.00–150.00.

LADY'S FACE • Yellow gold pin and mount of a lady's right profile carved in carnelian, pin marked "18K," late Victorian era. $100.00–175.00.

LADY'S FACE • Yellow gold pin and mount of a lady's right profile carved in high relief pink coral, late Victorian era. $100.00–175.00.

MYTHOLOGY • Yellow gold pin and mount with a carving in sardonyx of Zeus' eagle feeding from a bowl held by the seated Grecian goddess, Hebe, mid-Victorian era. $300.00–500.00.

LADY'S FACE • Yellow gold pin and mount of a lady's left profile carved in high relief pink coral, late Victorian era. $100.00–175.00.

WARRIOR'S FACE • Yellow gold pin and mount of a warrior's left profile carved in white on black onyx, mid-Victorian era. $75.00–150.00.

QUEEN VICTORIA • Yellow gold pin and mount of Queen Victoria's left profile carved in white on black onyx, pin is marked "14K," mid-Victorian era. $75.00–150.00.

SECOND ROW *(left to right)*

LADY'S FACE • Gold-plated pin and dangled mount of a lady's left profile carved in shell, late Victorian era. $35.00–50.00.

WARRIOR'S FACE • Yellow gold pin and mount of a warrior's right profile carved in shell, mid-Victorian era. $100.00–150.00.

LADY'S FACE • White gold pin and mount of a lady's right profile carved in white on black onyx, pin marked "14K," Art Deco era. $100.00–150.00.

LADY'S FACE • Yellow gold pin and mount of a lady's left profile carved in very high relief pink and white coral, late Victorian era. $150.00–250.00.

LADY'S FACE • White gold pin and mount of a lady's right profile carved in shell, late Victorian era. $100.00–150.00.

LADY'S FACE • Yellow gold pin and mount of a lady's left profile carved in white on blue-green onyx, late Victorian era. $75.00–150.00.

LADY'S FACE • Yellow gold pin and mount with the front view of a lady's face in high relief carved in coral, pin marked "10K," late Victorian era. $50.00–75.00.

THIRD ROW *(left to right)*

MYTHOLOGY • Yellow gold pin and mount of a white on green image of Cupid, reverse is marked "Wedgwood," pin marked "10K," late Victorian era. $50.00–100.00.

MYTHOLOGY • White gold pin and mount of a white on blue image of a Greek god, reverse is marked "Wedgwood," late Victorian era. $100.00–150.00.

LADY'S FACE • Gold-plated pin and mount of a lady's very high relief front view carved in lava, late Victorian era. $100.00–175.00.

LADY'S FACE • Gold-plated pin and mount of a lady's very high relief left front view carved in lava, late Victorian era. $150.00–200.00.

WARRIOR'S FACE • Brass pin and mount of a warrior's left profile molded in mud-colored imitation lava, late Victorian era. $35.00–50.00.

MYTHOLOGY • Yellow gold pin and mount of a Greek goddess in full front figure carved in white on black onyx, pin marked "10K," late Victorian era. $100.00–150.00.

MYTHOLOGY • White gold pin and mount in the figure of a Greek cherub playing a horn and carved in sardonyx, late Victorian era. $100.00–150.00.

FOURTH ROW *(left to right)*

WARRIOR'S FACE • Yellow gold pin and mount of a warrior's right profile carved in bloodstone, late Victorian era. $100.00–150.00.

STEEPLECHASE • Yellow gold pin and mount with the image of a horse and rider jumping a fence in white on black Wedgwood, late Victorian era. $50.00–100.00.

LADY'S FACE • White gold pin and mount of a lady's right profile carved in white onyx, late Victorian era. $50.00–100.00.

WOLF'S HEAD • Yellow gold pin and mount of a wolf's right profile carved in sardonyx, face of wolf badly worn, probably early Victorian era. $50.00–75.00.

LADY'S FACE • Yellow gold pin and mount of a lady's right profile carved in white onyx, late Victorian era. $50.00–75.00.

CARIBOU • Yellow gold pin and mount in the full figure of a caribou facing left made of white on dark blue Wedgwood, late Victorian era. $50.00–100.00.

LADY'S FACE • Yellow gold pin and mount of a lady's left profile carved in shell, late Victorian era. $100.00–150.00.

FIFTH ROW *(left to right)*

LADY'S FACE • Gold-filled pin and mount of a lady's right profile carved in tigereye, late Victorian era. $50.00–125.00.

LADY'S FACE • Yellow gold pin and mount of a lady's right profile carved in shell, pin marked "G.C.H & Co." (G.C. Hudson Co., Attleboro, Mass.) and "10K," circa 1915. $50.00–75.00.

LADY'S FACE • Yellow gold pin and mount of a lady's right profile carved in shell, late Victorian era. $50.00–75.00.

MYTHOLOGY • Yellow gold pin and mount of a high relief figure of a Grecian goddess with a lyre carved in black lava, late Victorian era. $150.00–200.00.

LADY'S FACE • Rose gold pin and yellow gold mount of a lady's face in very high relief carved in lava, late Victorian era. $150.00–200.00.

REBECCA AT THE WELL • Yellow gold pin and mount of Rebecca carved in shell, late Victorian era. $50.00–75.00.

LADY'S FACE • Yellow gold pin and mount of a lady's right profile in a rectangular carving of white on black onyx, late Victorian era. $75.00–150.00.

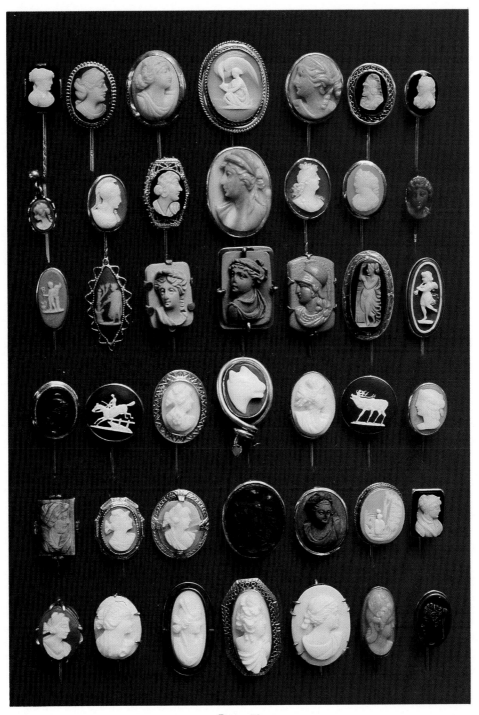

PLATE 12

SIXTH ROW *(left to right)*

LADY'S FACE • Silver pin and mount of a lady's right profile carved in shell, pin marked "STERLING," late Victorian era. $35.00–50.00.

LADY'S FACE • Silver pin and mount of a lady's very high relief right profile carved in white coral, late Victorian era. $35.00–50.00.

LADY'S FACE • Sterling silver pin and mount with the long oval right profile of a lady carved in white coral, late Victorian era. $50.00–75.00.

LADY'S FACE • Yellow gold pin and gold filigree mount of a lady's very high relief right profile carved in white and pink coral, pin marked "10K," late Victorian era. $150.00–200.00.

LADY'S FACE • Sterling silver pin and mount of a lady's right profile carved in white coral, late Victorian era. $75.00–125.00.

LADY'S FACE • Yellow gold pin and mount of a lady's right profile molded in colored glass, Art Deco era. $25.00–50.00.

MAN'S FACE • Yellow gold pin and mount of a man's left profile die-cast in silver on a red dyed metal background, Art Deco era. $25.00–50.00.

CARVINGS

Stickpins listed in this category may be evaluated from more than a single perspective. Not only are they rare pieces of antique jewelry, but like cameos and painted portraits, they are collectible pieces of beautiful art work exemplifying the talents of the artisans who created them.

The myriad of motifs and the various materials used in these works are many, and these factors, together with the quality of workmanship, should be considered when establishing a stickpin's value.

When all features are taken into account, it is not difficult to understand why some of the pieces in this category may rank among the most fascinating in this entire collection. We believe you will agree when you examine these shown here.

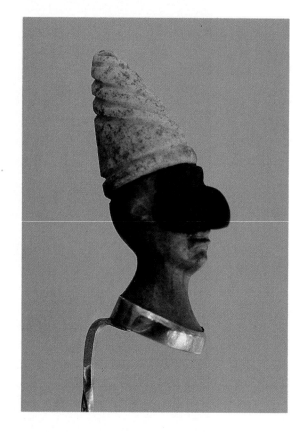

MASKED ACTOR • *Yellow gold pin and mount holding the three-dimensional likeness of a masked Elizabethan actor's head carved from granite, lava, and jet, the pin has an unidentified hallmark, mid-Victorian era.* $300.00–400.00.

PLATE 13

TOP ROW *(left to right)*

CHERUB • Yellow gold pin mounted with a full-figured cherub in right profile carved from tortoise shell, late Victorian era. $100.00–250.00.

CHRIST • Yellow gold pin mounted with the left profile of Jesus Christ carved in opal, late Victorian era. $200.00–350.00.

BABY'S FACE • Yellow gold pin and mount holding a moonstone carving of a baby's face topped with a silver bonnet set with nine graduated rose-cut diamonds and a gold bow tied under the chin, mid-Victorian era. $300.00–600.00.

MADONNA • Yellow gold pin mounted with the left profile of the Madonna carved in opal, late Victorian era. $125.00–250.00.

HORSE HEAD • Silver pin and yellow gold mount holding a three-dimensional likeness of a horse's head carved from tigereye and set with glass eyes, late Victorian era. $100.00–200.00.

SECOND ROW *(left to right)*

ROSE • Yellow gold pin mounted with a carved ivory rose, late Victorian era. $35.00–50.00.

MAN'S FACE • Gold-plated pin mounted with the front view of an Oriental man's face carved from angel-skin coral, late Victorian era. $125.00–200.00.

SCARF PIN • Yellow gold pin and mount holding a three-dimensional likeness of a raised hand carved from red coral and holding a gold dagger, late Victorian era. $150.00–300.00.

BOUQUET • Yellow gold pin and mount set with a floral bouquet carved from pink coral, late Victorian era. $125.00–200.00.

ROSE • Yellow gold pin and mount holding a rose carved from red coral, late Victorian era. $35.00–50.00.

THIRD ROW *(left to right)*

HEREFORD • Silver pin and yellow gold mount holding a front view of a whiteface Hereford's head carved from ivory and set with glass eyes, late Victorian era. $100.00–175.00.

LADY'S FACE • Yellow gold pin mounted with the right profile of a lady carved in white coral, late Victorian era. $125.00–200.00.

CHINESE MAN • Yellow gold pin and mount holding a three-dimensional head carving of a Chinese man carved from ivory, late Victorian era. $225.00–300.00.

INDIAN • Gold-plated pin mounted with a front view of an Indian chieftain's head carved from bone, late Victorian era. $35.00–50.00.

DOG • Gold-plated pin mounted with a front view of a bulldog's head carved from bone, Victorian era. $35.00–50.00.

FOURTH ROW *(left to right)*

COLUMBUS • Yellow gold pin and mount holding a three-dimensional bust of Columbus carved from lava and set with 10 rose-cut diamonds plus two that are missing, mid-Victorian era. $300.00–600.00.

PLATE 13

ELEPHANT • Silver pin mounted with the front view of an elephant's head carved from ivory, late Victorian era. $100.00–175.00.

BACCHUS • Yellow gold pin and mount holding the front view of the head of Bacchus, the Roman god of wine, carved from labradorite and set with rose-cut diamond eyes, mid-Victorian era. $600.00–800.00.

DOG • Yellow gold pin mounted with the left profile of a wolfhound carved from bone, late Victorian era. $35.00–50.00.

SOCRATES • Gold-plated pin mounted with the three-dimensional profile of the famous Greek philosopher carved from lava. Bust is signed on reverse "INVERNO," late Victorian era. $150.00–250.00.

FIFTH ROW (left to right)

MAN'S FACE • Yellow gold pin and Tiffany type mount holding a full front close-up of a man's face carved from jet, late Victorian era. $35.00–75.00.

FISH • Yellow gold pin mounted with the full-length replica of a fish carved from ivory, late Victorian era. $50.00–75.00.

INDIAN • Yellow gold pin mounted with the face of an Indian chieftain carved from ivory, late Victorian era. $50.00–75.00.

DOG • Gold-plated pin mounted with the full figure of a spaniel in left profile carved from ivory, late Victorian era. $50.00–75.00.

ROSE • Yellow gold pin mounted with the likeness of a blooming rose carved from pink coral, late Victorian era. $35.00–50.00.

CELTIC AND NATIVE AMERICAN

Because both Celtic and Native American stickpins are somewhat limited in this collection, we have combined the two categories. Although these two ethnic groups are separated by several thousand miles, their jewelry items have certain similarities. Silver was used extensively by both the Celts and the American Indian, and both feature stones found in their immediate habitat.

While the Scottish "pebble" jewelry was commonly inlaid with stones from the Cairngorm mountains of Scotland, the silver creations of the Indian nations of the Southwest were mostly graced with turquoise from the deserts of the United States. Then too, both of these nationalities looked to nature for their design motifs, featuring the flora and fauna of their native homelands.

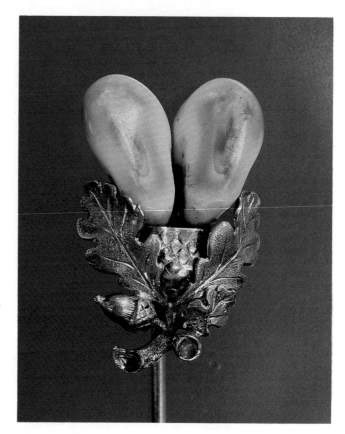

SCOTTISH • *Yellow gold pin and mount in acorn and oak leaf motif set with a 2mm, rose-cut, pink quartz stone and two stag's teeth, reverse of mount is engraved with the date "26-2-12" (February 26, 1912), mount is also marked "585" followed by an unidentified hallmark, circa 1912. $100.00–150.00.*

PLATE 14

FIRST ROW (*left to right*)

SCOTTISH • Yellow gold pin and shield-shaped mount set with flat pieces of bloodstone and Scotch agate, mid-Victorian era. $75.00–100.00.

SCOTTISH • Yellow gold pin and mount with acorns and green enameled oak leaves and set with two stag's teeth, pin is marked "585," mid-Victorian era. $75.00–100.00.

SCOTTISH • Sterling silver pin and an engraved shield-shaped mount set with a 9mm cairngorm (sometimes called "Scotch topaz") and surrounded by six 3mm stones of garnet, amethyst, citrine, and amber, circa 1865. $150.00–200.00.

SCOTTISH • Yellow gold pin and mount with inlaid enameled acorns and oak leaves and set with two stag's teeth, mid-Victorian era. $100.00–150.00.

SCOTTISH • Sterling silver pin and shield-shaped mount set with flat pieces of bloodstone and Scotch agate, mid-Victorian era. $50.00–75.00.

SECOND ROW (*left to right*)

SCOTTISH • Sterling silver pin and dirk (dagger) mount set with cairngorm, bloodstone, and Scotch agate, mid-Victorian era. $50.00–75.00.

SCOTTISH • Silver pin and gold-plated leaf and thistle mount set with an amethyst, mid-Victorian era. $25.00–50.00.

IRISH • Sterling silver pin and an engraved Irish harp mount inlaid with flat pieces of serpentine, reverse of mount is marked by the maker, "S & Co" and followed by the hallmarks of an anchor, a lion, and the letter "h" signifying it was made in Birmingham, England, in 1907. $200.00–300.00.

SCOTTISH • Sterling silver pin with an oak leaf and thistle mount set with an amethyst, mid-Victorian era. $50.00–75.00.

SCOTTISH • Sterling silver pin and horseshoe-shaped mount set with flat pieces of bloodstone and Scotch agate, mid-Victorian era. $35.00–50.00.

THIRD ROW (*left to right*)

INDIAN • Silver pin mounted with an engraved silver moccasin, Art Deco era. $35.00–50.00.

INDIAN HEAD • Gold-filled pin and mount of an Indian brave's face, Art Deco era. $25.00–45.00.

INDIAN HEAD • Gold plated on copper pin and mount of an Indian chieftain's face, Art Deco era. $25.00–45.00.

INDIAN HEAD • Gold-plated pin and mount of an Indian maiden's left profile set with three mine-cut rhinestones in her headband, Art Deco era. $35.00–50.00.

INDIAN HEAD • Gold-plated pin and disc mount with an Indian brave's left profile in relief, Art Deco era. $25.00–45.00.

PLATE 14

FOURTH ROW (*left to right*)

INDIAN HEAD • Gold-plated pin and mount of an Indian brave shown in right profile with an enameled face and a peace pipe in his mouth, Art Deco era. (Pin is in poor condition.) $10.00–15.00.

ARROWHEAD • Yellow gold pin and mount holding an authentic flint bird-point, probably mid-Victorian era. $75.00–100.00.

ARROWHEAD • Yellow gold pin and mount holding an authentic flint head, probably mid-Victorian era. $75.00–100.00.

ARROWHEAD • Yellow gold pin and mount holding a small bird-point, probably mid-Victorian period. $75.00–100.00.

INDIAN HEAD • Gold-plated pin and mount of an Indian chieftain's right profile set with a rhinestone in his neckpiece, Art Deco era. $10.00–20.00.

FIFTH ROW (*left to right*)

SWASTIKA • Gold-filled pin and mount engraved with an Indian four-pointed star and arrows, pin is marked "W & Co" (Weinman & Co., Philadelphia, PA), circa 1904. $20.00–35.00.

ZUNI • Silver pin and bird-shaped mount inset with turquoise, reverse is marked "25," Art Deco era. $20.00–35.00.

ARROWHEAD • Yellow gold pin and mount holding a white quartz arrowhead, probably mid-Victorian era. $75.00–100.00.

ZUNI • Silver pin and mount of an Indian sunburst inset with pieces of pearl, onyx, turquoise, and agate, marked on reverse with maker's symbol, Art Deco era. $20.00–35.00.

ZUNI • Silver pin and mount of a blue enameled swastika showing Indian star-burst and arrows, Art Deco era. $20.00–30.00.

COINS

From the time when governments first began issuing bits of metal as a medium of exchange, people have been using coins to adorn themselves in one way or another. Some of these early pieces of money bore the likenesses of ancient gods or emperors and were thought to bring protection and good fortune when utilized to grace armor and weapons of warriors.

Coins, both ancient and those of more recent mintage, were also used as the motif for stickpins from the Georgian era until the days when wearing them became passé. Many coins, prized highly by numismatic scholars, were ruined when converted into jewelry pieces. If the coin is in its original state, mounted in a protective bezel, the pin may be worth more than coins that have been defaced in the mounting process.

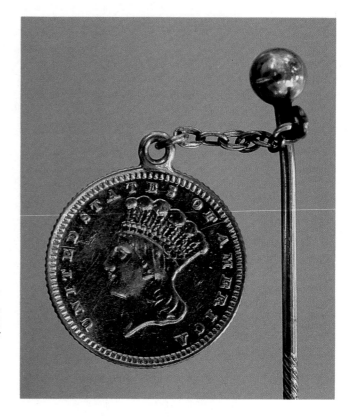

UNITED STATES COIN • *Yellow gold pin dangling a "Crowned Liberty" 1861 U.S. gold dollar, reverse has been polished and engraved with the entwined initials "TGD" for Theodore and Gertrude Debs, brother and sister-in-law of Eugene V. Debs, several-time candidate for President of the United States on the Socialist ticket, circa 1880. $100.00–150.00.*

PLATE 15

UPPER ARCH *(left to right)*

NEWFOUNDLAND • Silver pin with five-cent piece bearing the likeness of Edward VII. The crown was added when the coin was converted to a stickpin, Edwardian era. $25.00–45.00.

REPUBLIC DE PANAMA • Silver pin and 1907 coin with the likeness of Balboa in repoussé, pin is mounted directly to the reverse of the coin, Edwardian era. $25.00–45.00.

UNITED STATES • Silver pin and 1908 ten-cent piece with the face of Liberty in repoussé, mount is marked "Pat Nov 22 1904,"circa 1908. $25.00–45.00.

UNITED STATES • Silver pin and 1903 twenty-five cent piece with the face of Liberty in repoussé, mount is marked "Pat Nov 22, 1904," circa 1904. $35.00–50.00.

UNITED STATES • Silver pin and 1908 five-cent piece with the face of an Indian chief in repoussé, mount is marked "Pat Nov 22 1904," circa 1908. $25.00–45.00.

UNITED STATES • Copper pin and one-cent piece with the face of Lincoln in repoussé, pin is mounted directly to the reverse of the coin, circa 1900. $25.00–45.00.

GREAT BRITAIN • Silver pin and 1887 three-penny bit with the likeness of Queen Victoria, pin is mounted directly to the reverse of the coin, late Victorian era. $15.00–25.00.

SECOND ARCH *(left to right)*

CALIFORNIA • Yellow gold pin and 1849 octagon gold dollar with likeness of an Indian chief, pin is mounted directly to the reverse of the coin, late Victorian era. $25.00–45.00.

CALIFORNIA • Yellow gold pin and 1849 round gold dollar with likeness of an Indian chief, pin is mounted directly to the reverse of the coin, late Victorian era. $25.00–45.00.

UNITED STATES • Yellow gold pin and 1925 2½ dollar gold piece with an eagle on front and Indian chief on reverse, pin is mounted directly to the reverse of the coin, circa 1925. $150.00–200.00.

ALASKA • Yellow gold pin and 1909 gold half dollar with likeness of a prospector, pin is mounted directly to the reverse of the coin, circa 1909. $25.00–45.00.

UNITED STATES • Yellow gold pin dangling a "Crowned Liberty" 1861 U.S. gold dollar, circa 1861. $100.00–150.00.

THIRD ARCH *(left to right)*

GREECE • Yellow gold pin and bezel mount holding ancient bronze Delmatius of about 335 A.D., late Victorian era. $100.00–150.00.

GREECE • Silver pin and bezel mount holding ancient silver piece with the likeness of Greek god, late Victorian era. $75.00–100.00.

ROMAN • 14K yellow gold pin and bezel mount holding a silver coin with the likeness of the Emperor Antoninus Pius (138-161 A.D.), late Victorian era. $125.00–175.00.

PLATE 15

ROMAN • Silver pin and bezel mount holding an ancient Denarius of about 200 B.C. with the likeness of Meta and the reverse marked "ROMA," Edwardian era. $75.00–100.00.

GREECE • Silver pin set into the bottom of an ancient Corinthian coin, Edwardian era. $50.00–75.00.

BOTTOM ARCH *(left to right)*

FRENCH MEDALLION • Gold-plated pin and bezel holding a small gold commemorative coin with the likeness of Napoleon, Edwardian era. $50.00–100.00.

UNITED STATES • Yellow gold pin and 1892 ten-cent piece dangling from a ring mounted on top of coin. Reverse of coin has been polished smooth, engraved in floral motif, and set with red, white, and blue glass beads, Edwardian era. $50.00–75.00.

BRITISH MEDALLION • Yellow gold pin and commemorative medallion depicting St. George slaying a dragon, pin is fixed directly to the reverse of the coin, Edwardian era. $75.00–125.00.

CORAL

Coral is actually the massed projections of tiny marine animals occurring in branched, tree-like shapes found in the waters of the oceans. It may even be valued as high or higher than some gemstones, and comes in colors ranging from a whitish pink through shades of oranges and reds to a near black.

The ancient Romans believed that coral held the power to heal afflictions of various types, and for centuries, it has been used for decorative purposes by peoples of all nations. Even the Native Americans of the southwestern United States still use it in their silver works as they have for countless generations. In fact, coral is a common medium in creating all types of jewelry, and was used extensively during the Victorian Era.

In stickpins, it is most often seen in cameos and floral carvings, but it may also be found in its natural state when branched pieces are set in gold or silver mounts.

BRANCH CORAL • *Yellow gold pin and mount set with a natural branch of orange coral, late Victorian era. $75.00–100.00.*

PLATE 16

FIRST ARCH *(left to right)*

FLORAL MOTIF • Yellow gold pin and mount set with four oval cabochon pieces of orange coral and a single seed pearl, late Victorian era. $25.00–50.00.

CAMEO MOTIF • Gold-plated pin and oval mount set with a faux coral cameo of a lady's face, late Victorian era. $20.00–35.00.

ORIENTAL MOTIF • Gold-plated pin and oval mount embossed with Oriental characters and chrysanthemums and set with an oval cabochon piece of imitation angel-skin coral, late Victorian era. $20.00–35.00.

NATURAL • Gold-filled pin and mount set with a branch of orange-colored coral, late Victorian era. $45.00–75.00.

FLORAL MOTIF • Yellow gold pin and leaf mount set with a carved orange-colored coral blossom, late Victorian era. $75.00–100.00.

NATURAL • Yellow gold pin and heart-shaped mount set with a branch of orange coral, late Victorian era. $45.00–75.00.

CAMEO • Gold-filled pin and embossed mount set with an oval coral carving of a lady's right profile, mid-Victorian era. $45.00–75.00.

CAMEO • Yellow gold pin and mount set with an oval imitation coral cameo of lady's right profile and 2mm mine-cut rhinestone, late Victorian era. $25.00–45.00.

FLORAL MOTIF • Sterling silver pin and mount set with a pink coral bead and six baroque pearls, late Victorian era. $35.00–50.00.

SHOWN AT LEFT AND RIGHT

CARVING • Yellow gold pin with a high relief carving of a lady's face in orange coral, late Victorian era. $50.00–75.00.

CARVING • Gold-plated pin and mount set with a carving of a lady's face in orange coral, late Victorian era. $50.00–75.00.

SECOND ARCH *(left to right)*

IMITATION CORAL • Yellow gold pin and mount set with a round piece of faux coral, late Victorian era. $25.00–40.00.

FLORAL MOTIF • Yellow gold pin with a high relief carving of a flower in orange coral, late Victorian era. $45.00–75.00.

ANGEL-SKIN • Gold-filled pin and embossed mount set with an oval cabochon piece of angel-skin coral, late Victorian era. $45.00–75.00.

BRANCH CORAL • Yellow gold pin and mount set with a natural branch of orange coral, late Victorian era. (Note: This same stickpin is shown in the category lead photo.) $75.00–100.00.

CAMEO • Gold-filled pin and inlaid enameled mount with a lady's left profile molded in imitation pink coral, late Victorian era. $25.00–45.00.

CABOCHON CUT • Silver pin and mount set with an oval piece of pink coral, reverse of mount marked "STERLING YALO," Art Nouveau period. $25.00–45.00.

CAMEO • Yellow gold pin and mount with a small carving of a lady's face in pink coral, pin is marked "F.P. CO." (Ford, Perry, & Co., Providence, RI), circa 1915. $45.00–75.00.

PLATE 16

BOTTOM ARCH *(left to right)*

SCARF • Yellow gold pin set with a teardrop of angel-skin coral, late Victorian era. $45.00–75.00.

FLORAL MOTIF • Yellow gold pin and flower mount holding a rose carved in orange coral and set with a half pearl, late Victorian era. $45.00–75.00.

SCARF PIN • Yellow gold pin and mount set with a teardrop of angel-skin coral and two seed pearls, pin is marked "14K," late Victorian era. $45.00–75.00.

CRESCENTS AND STARS

Often used as motifs in stickpins are planets and stars that have been observed by man since his origin. Scholars of ancient times studied the heavens and were awed by what they saw. In their imagination, the patterns formed by stars and planets in the galaxies took on the forms of their gods and the animals and objects that were common to their everyday lives.

Legends, myths, sorcery, and magic were all associated with the various constellations to such an extent that there are many who closely relate to their horoscopes even today. Hence, it is not surprising that crescents and stars have been adopted as good-luck symbols, logos for companies and fraternal organizations, and designs for all types of jewelry, including stickpins.

CRESCENT AND STAR • *Yellow gold pin and mount of a crescent set with three 3mm mine-cut rhinestones and a star set with one single-cut rhinestone, late Victorian era. $45.00–75.00.*

PLATE 17

UPPER ARCH (*left to right*)

CRESCENT AND STAR • Yellow gold pin and mount of a crescent set with five seed pearls and four Persian turquoise beads, and a star set with a small pearl, late Victorian era. $45.00–75.00.

CRESCENT AND STAR • Yellow gold pin and mount of a crescent set with 11 seed pearls, and a star is set with a small pearl, late Victorian era. $45.00–75.00.

CRESCENT AND LEAF • Gold-plated pin and mount of a moon with a yellow gold leaf set with a 2mm single-cut garnet, late Victorian era. $25.00–45.00.

CRESCENT • Yellow gold pin and mount of a crescent set with 11 graduated baroque pearls, late Victorian era. $45.00–75.00.

CRESCENT, ARROW, AND STAR • Yellow gold pin and mount of a gold arrow, crescent set with 11 Persian turquoise beads, and a star set with a seed pearl, late Victorian era. $100.00–150.00.

CRESCENT • Yellow gold pin and mount of a crescent moon channel set with eight graduated seed pearls and a small opal, late Victorian era. $45.00–75.00.

CRESCENT AND GNOME • Yellow gold pin and mount of a moon with a gnome astride the crescent while playing a pipe, set with 12 graduated seed pearls late Victorian era. $100.00–150.00.

CRESCENT • Yellow gold pin and mount of a crescent overlaid with mother-of-pearl and set with a 2mm single-cut blue stone, late Victorian era. $25.00–45.00.

CRESCENT AND FLOWER • Yellow gold pin and mount of a crescent and a flower, moon is set with seven baroque seed pearls, pin is marked "10K," late Victorian era. $35.00–50.00.

SHOWN AT LEFT AND RIGHT

CRESCENT • Yellow gold pin and mount of a crescent set with seven seed pearls, pin is marked "14K," late Victorian era. $50.00–75.00.

CRESCENT AND STAR • Yellow gold pin and mount, star is set with a 2mm brilliant cut diamond, Edwardian era. $75.00–100.00.

CENTER ARCH (*left to right*)

CRESCENT AND FLOWER • Yellow gold pin and mount, crescent is set with seven baroque seed pearls, while the flower is enameled and set with a single pearl, late Victorian era. $45.00–75.00.

CRESCENT AND BIRD • Yellow gold pin and mount, crescent is set with four seed pearls (with one missing), bird is set with two seed pearls and with a 2mm single-cut ruby in its beak, late Victorian era. $45.00–75.00.

CRESCENT AND FOUR-LEAF CLOVER • Yellow gold pin and mount, crescent is set with nine 2mm mine-cut diamonds and the clover is set with a 2mm mine-cut ruby, late Victorian era. $100.00–125.00.

PLATE 17

CRESCENT AND STAR • Yellow gold pin and mount set with four rhinestones, one blue, one green, and two clear, late Victorian era. $45.00–75.00.

STARBURST CRESCENT AND STAR • Two yellow gold pins with mounts connected by a gold chain, starburst is set with 25 seed pearls, crescent is set with seven seed pearls, and star is set with one seed pearl, both pins are marked "14K," late Victorian era. $150.00–200.00.

CRESCENT AND MAPLE LEAF • Yellow gold pin and mount, crescent is set with four seed pearls and a 2mm mine-cut ruby, pin is marked "10K," late Victorian era. $45.00–75.00.

BOTTOM ARCH (*left to right*)

CRESCENT • Yellow gold pin and mount, crescent is set with 11 seed pearls around a black enameled inner-crescent lettered in gold "1921," reverse of mount is marked "FULL GOLD," circa 1921. $45.00–75.00.

STAR AND SPIKE • Yellow gold pin and mount, star is set with 11 seed pearls, spike's head is set with a 2mm rose-cut diamond, reverse of mount is marked with "14K" and a hallmark, late Victorian era. $75.00–100.00.

CRESCENT AND STAR • Gold-plated pin and mount, crescent is set with seven seed pearls, star is set with a rose-cut garnet, late Victorian era. $45.00–75.00.

CROWNS AND FLEUR-DE-LIS

For centuries, the crown has been symbolic of an imperial state and, as such, has been worn as a part of the regalia of kings and queens of many nations. In England, even the coin of the realm is known as a "crown."

At the same time, just across the English Channel, the fleur-de-lis has been the emblem of France since it was first adopted by Louis VII in the year 1179. Later, in 1365, it was Charles V who first used three "flowers-of-the-iris" on his country's flag.

In England and in France, the crown and the fleur-de-lis have been worn into battle on the shields and breastplates of their armies. The two insignias were not only used as representative emblems of the two nations but were to become popular jewelry motifs as well. Today, they are among the most commonly found stickpin designs.

CROWN AND FLEUR-DE-LIS • *Gold-plated pin and crown-shaped mount set with six single-cut rhinestones. Fleur-de-lis is gold filled with a single seed pearl. Both are late Victorian era. $25.00–45.00 each.*

PLATE 18

UPPER ARCH *(left to right)*

FLEUR-DE-LIS • Yellow gold pin and mount, pin is marked "14K," late Victorian era. $40.00–60.00.

FLEUR-DE-LIS • Gold-plated pin with a fleur-de-lis shaped mother-of-pearl mount inlaid with shell, Edwardian era. $20.00–40.00.

FLEUR-DE-LIS • Gold-plated pin and mount pavé set with Persian turquoise, mid-Victorian era. $45.00–75.00.

FLEUR-DE-LIS • Yellow gold pin and mount with a gold crown and a Prince of Wales feather crest on royal blue enameled background, pin is marked "ICH DIEN" ("I SERVE"), late Victorian era. $45.00–75.00.

FLEUR-DE-LIS • Yellow gold pin and mount forming a crown, set with four seed pearls and a Prince of Wales feather crest, late Victorian era. $45.00–75.00.

FLEUR-DE-LIS • Silver pin and mount inlaid with royal blue enamel, pin is marked "STERLING," late Victorian era. $25.00–45.00.

FLEUR-DE-LIS • Yellow gold pin and mount set with 10 pearls, late Victorian era. $35.00–60.00.

SECOND ARCH *(left to right)*

SMALL FLEUR-DE-LIS • Yellow gold pin and mount set with nine seed pearls, reverse of mount is marked "14K" with the letters "GS" inside of a diamond, late Victorian era. $45.00–75.00.

FLEUR-DE-LIS • Yellow gold pin and mount set with three pearls and two rose-cut rubies, late Victorian era. $45.00–75.00.

DISK AND CROWN • Silver pin mounted with a silver crown and open Bible superimposed on a silver disk that is lettered in royal blue enamel "FEARE GOD HONOR YE KINGE," reverse of disk is marked with the letter "M," an anchor, and lion, and "KD" followed by the number "50967." The marks show that the pin was made in Birmingham in 1886. $45.00–75.00.

FLEUR-DE-LIS • Yellow gold pin and mount set with a pearl and white and blue inlaid enameled flowers, pin is marked "14K," late Victorian era. $45.00–75.00.

FLEUR-DE-LIS • Yellow gold pin and mount inlaid with light blue enamel, late Victorian era. $35.00–50.00.

THIRD ROW *(left to right)*

SHIELD AND CROWN • Silver pin mounted with a silver crown topped shield with three silver crowns on a basse-taille royal blue enameled background, reverse is marked "925" and "ABH," late Victorian era. $35.00–50.00.

CREST AND CROWN • Silver pin and mount of a crown topped with a red, white, and blue crest lettered "GR VI." This was probably used in commemoration of the coronation of King George VI, circa 1936. $35.00–50.00.

CROWN • Extra long silver pin and a large relief mount of a silver crown set with a Mexican turquoise bead, marked on reverse "TAXCO" and "980," Art Deco era. $25.00–45.00.

CREST AND CROWN • Silver pin and crown topped mount with a raised flower and the letters "FY," late Victorian era. $25.00–45.00.

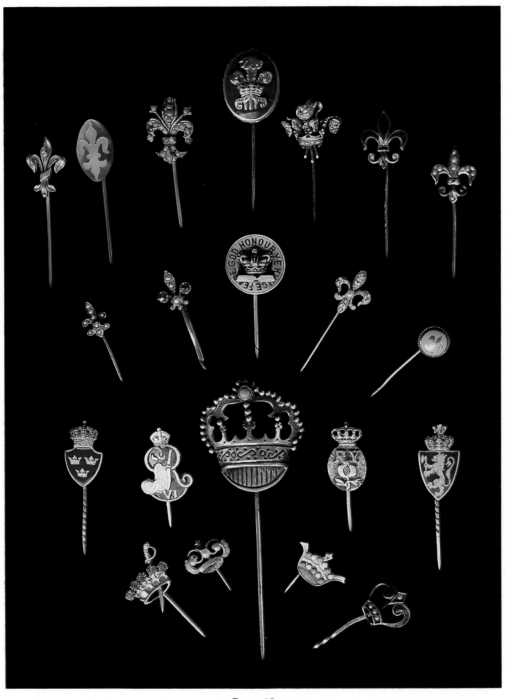

PLATE 18

CREST AND CROWN • Silver pin and mount of a crown topped shield with basse-taille scarlet enamel and a silver rampant lion with a battle ax, late Victorian era. $35.00–50.00.

LOWER ARCH *(left to right)*

CROWN AND SABER • Gilded pin and mount set with five rhinestones, Edwardian era. $25.00–45.00.

CROWN • Yellow gold pin and mount set with three pearls and inlaid with red and green enamel, pin is marked "10K," Edwardian era. $45.00–60.00.

CROWN • Gilded pin and inlaid blue enamel mount set with six turquoise and five white beads with blue enamel, Edwardian era. $25.00–45.00.

CROWN • Yellow gold pin and mount finished in basse-taille enamel and set with four pearls, Edwardian era. $35.00–50.00.

DEMONS, DRAGONS, AND REPTILES

Through fossil remains, we know that 100 million years ago, giant dinosaurs lived on this planet. Writings of the Old Testament refer to Lucifer, the fallen angel, who as Satan, took the form of the serpent in the Garden of Eden. Then there were the legends of the Middle Ages that told of dreadful, fire-breathing monsters called dragons with great bat-like wings, horns, and terrible talons.

So, it is not surprising that demons, dragons, and reptiles would be among the subjects used in jewelry creations. The snake, for instance, was a symbol of eternity and was extremely popular in the jewelry of the early Victorian era. Mounted on a stickpin, it is often found coiled around a gemstone with its head down.

Stickpins in this category, while not rare, are not found quite as often as some of the other motifs.

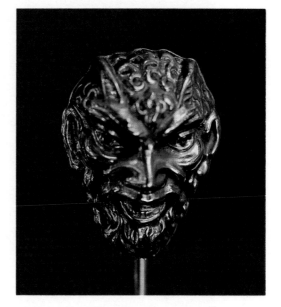

SATAN • *Yellow gold pin and mount shaped in the likeness of the Devil's face, reverse is marked "10K," Art Deco era. $100.00–150.00.*

PLATE 19

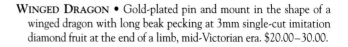

FIRST ROW *(left to right)*

FLYING DRAGON • Silver pin and mount in the shape of a winged dragon, reverse is stamped, "STERLING" and hallmarked "L & A" in circles (Link & Angell, Newark, New Jersey), circa 1900. $25.00–45.00.

FLYING DRAGON • Yellow gold pin and mount in the shape of a winged dragon with rose-cut ruby eye and gripping a pearl in its talons, reverse marked "14K" and hallmarked "L & A" in linked circles (Link & Angell, Newark, New Jersey), circa 1900. $45.00–75.00.

DRAGON • Gold-filled pin and oval mount set with faceted amethyst and guarded by a gold dragon, mid-Victorian era. $45.00–75.00.

FLYING DRAGON • Yellow gold pin and mount in the shape of a winged dragon with a single-cut ruby eye, reverse is marked "14K," mid-Victorian era. $45.00–75.00.

FLYING DRAGON • Yellow gold pin and mount in the shape of a winged dragon with its body pierced by a lance, mid-Victorian era. $45.00–75.00.

SECOND ROW *(left to right)*

WINGED DRAGON • Gold-plated pin and mount in the shape of a winged dragon with a rose-cut ruby eye, mid-Victorian era. $25.00–45.00.

SIGNET • Yellow gold pin and mount in the shape of a shield engraved with an Old English letter "F" and guarded by a dragon, pin is marked "P.S.Co." (Plainville Stock Co., Plainville, Mass.), circa 1896. $25.00–45.00.

WINGED DRAGON • Brass pin and mount in the shape of a winged dragon with cabochon ruby eyes and set with a diamond-shaped citrine above its head, pin is marked "DUNN" (E.L. Dunn, Providence, Rhode Island), circa 1880. $35.00–60.00.

DRAGON • Gold-filled pin and mount in the shape of a dragon with a cabochon peridot eye and a 2mm single-cut diamond in its mouth, reverse of mount marked "GF" (Garland Fisher Co., Newark, N.J.), circa 1915. $45.00–75.00.

WINGED DRAGON • Gold-plated pin and mount in the shape of a winged dragon with long beak pecking at 3mm single-cut imitation diamond fruit at the end of a limb, mid-Victorian era. $20.00–30.00.

THIRD ROW *(left to right)*

WINGED DRAGON • Gold-plated pin and rose gold mount in the shape of a winged dragon with a Persian turquoise bead in its mouth and an arrow piercing its body, mid-Victorian era. $35.00–60.00.

SIGNET • Gold-filled pin and oval mount engraved with the script letter "R" and guarded by a winged dragon, mid-Victorian era. $25.00–45.00.

WINGED DRAGON • Gold plate on silver pin and mount set with a baroque pearl guarded by a winged dragon, the reverse is marked "STERLING" and hallmarked with the letter "S" in a circle (Shepard Mfg. Co., Melrose Highlands, Mass.), circa 1893. $25.00–45.00.

FLYING DRAGON • Yellow gold pin and mount in the shape of a flying dragon with a pearl in its mouth, mid-Victorian era. $35.00–60.00.

FLYING DRAGON • Yellow gold pin and mount in the shape of a flying dragon with a pearl in its mouth, reverse of mount is marked "14 A" in a clover leaf (Alling & Co., Newark, N.J.), circa 1896. $45.00–75.00.

FOURTH ROW *(left to right)*

SERPENT • Gold-filled pin and mount in the shape of a snake with a rose-cut red stone in its head, body is coiled around a pentagon red quartz stone, pin is marked "14K GF," mid-Victorian era. $35.00–60.00.

SERPENT • Gold-plated pin and mount in the shape of a snake coiled with its head up and with two red stone eyes, mid-Victorian era. $25.00–45.00.

SERPENT • Gold-plated pin and mount in the shape of a snake coiled head down around a diamond-shaped amethyst, late Victorian era. $25.00–45.00.

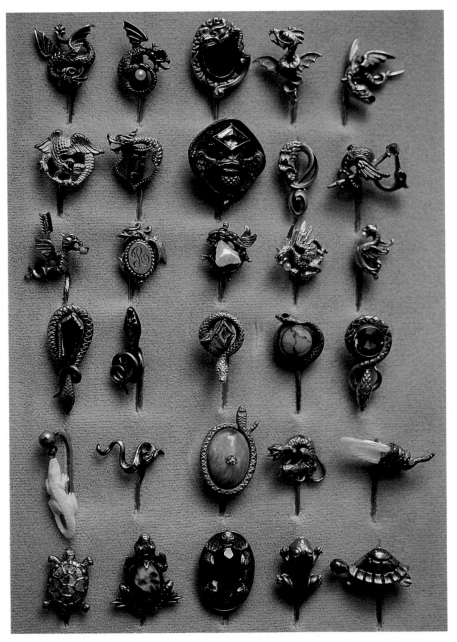

PLATE 19

SERPENT • Gold-plated pin and mount in the shape of a snake with a single-cut garnet eye and coiled head up around a bead of artificial turquoise, mid-Victorian era. $15.00–25.00.

SERPENT • Yellow gold pin and mount in the shape of a snake coiled head down around a 6mm European-cut topaz, mid-Victorian era. $50.00–100.00.

FIFTH ROW (*left to right*)

ALLIGATOR • Brass pin and mount dangling a carved bone likeness of an alligator, Art Deco era. $15.00–25.00.

SEA SERPENT • Brass pin and mount in the shape of a swimming serpent, Edwardian era. $15.00–25.00.

SERPENT • Gold-plated pin and mount shaped like a snake coiled head up around an oval cabochon of green glass with a 2mm rose-cut clear quartz stone, Edwardian era. $15.00–25.00.

LIZARD • Gold-plated pin and mount in the shape of a chuckwalla on a log, Edwardian era. $15.00–25.00.

SERPENT • Gold-plated pin and mount in the shape of a snake coiled around a pearl slug, Edwardian era. $15.00–25.00.

SIXTH ROW (*left to right*)

TURTLE • Gold tinted pin and a thin, stamped metal mount shaped like a turtle, Art Deco era. $2.00–8.00.

FROG • Silver pin and mount in the shape of a frog with its back set with piece of brown and white agate, Art Deco era. $15.00–25.00.

TURTLE • Gold-plated pin and oval mount in the likeness of a turtle, its back is set with oval faux topaz, Art Nouveau era. $25.00–45.00.

FROG • Gold washed pin and thin metal mount in the shape of a frog, Art Deco era. $1.00–5.00.

TURTLE • Copper pin and mount in the shape of a crawling turtle, Art Deco era. $10.00–15.00.

DIAMONDS

This category needs little or no introduction, for the diamond is the most popular of all gemstones. A crystal of pure carbon, it is clear and the hardest of all natural materials.

It is believed that the early Romans were the first to make use of this stone as an adornment to their armor. Because of the diamond's lasting quality in ancient times it was thought to be unconquerable and to possess the power to ward off all that was evil.

The diamond is the birthstone of April and has become the ultimate symbol of truth, love, and betrothal.

It is through the expertise of those who cut and polish the rough, newly-mined diamonds that their fire and brilliance is brought to life, and they are then used in creating some of the most exquisitely beautiful and expensive pieces of jewelry.

DIAMOND HORSESHOE • *Yellow gold pin and horseshoe motif mount set with a single 6mm brilliant-cut diamond, pin is marked "14K," Art Deco era. $300.00–500.00.*

PLATE 20

UPPER ARCH (*left to right*)

DIAMOND • White gold pin and filigree mount set with a 2mm single-cut diamond, pin marked "14K," late Victorian era. $100.00–150.00.

DIAMOND • White gold pin and mount set with a 2½mm mine-cut diamond, late Victorian era. $100.00–150.00.

DIAMOND • Yellow gold pin with a yellow gold and platinum mount set with a single 2½mm brilliant cut diamond, marked "14K-PLAT," Edwardian era. $125.00–175.00.

DIAMOND AND PERIDOT • Yellow gold pin with a yellow and white gold mount set with a 4mm square peridot, five 2mm to 3mm graduated brilliant cut diamonds, and a single pearl, Edwardian era. $200.00–300.00.

BOW MOTIF • Platinum pin and platinum bow motif mount set with a 2mm brilliant cut diamond and 20 smaller mine-cut diamonds, Edwardian era. $200.00–300.00.

WHITE SAPPHIRE • Yellow gold pin and white gold mount set with a pear-shaped stone, pin is marked "R & N - 14K," Art Deco era. (Note: Diamonds are often confused with white sapphires. Through error this pin is shown in the wrong category.) $150.00–200.00.

BELL MOTIF • White gold pin and bell-shaped mount set with six 2mm mine-cut diamonds and a 4mm cabochon sapphire clapper, Edwardian era. $200.00–300.00.

DIAMONDS • White gold pin and filigree mount set with one 3mm and one 2mm mine-cut diamond, pin is marked "14K," Edwardian era. $125.00–175.00.

DIAMOND AND RUBY • White gold pin and mount set with a 2mm brilliant cut diamond and a 3mm marquise-cut ruby, Edwardian era. $125.00–175.00.

SHOWN AT LEFT AND RIGHT

DIAMONDS • White gold pin and mount with a cluster of seven 3mm brilliant cut diamonds, Art Deco era. $400.00–700.00.

DIAMONDS • Yellow gold pin with a white gold mount set with eight 2mm mine-cut diamonds and one 2mm brilliant cut diamond, Edwardian era. $200.00–300.00.

LOWER ARCH (*left to right*)

DIAMOND • White gold pin and mount set with a 3mm single cut diamond in a modified Tiffany type mount, Art Deco era. $50.00–$100.00.

CIRCLE MOTIF • Rose gold pin and a rose gold circle mount set with ten 2mm rose-cut diamonds, mid-Victorian era. $100.00–150.00.

BOW MOTIF • Rose gold pin and bow-shaped mount set with six 2mm rose-cut and three 3mm mine-cut diamonds, mid-Victorian era. $100.00–150.00.

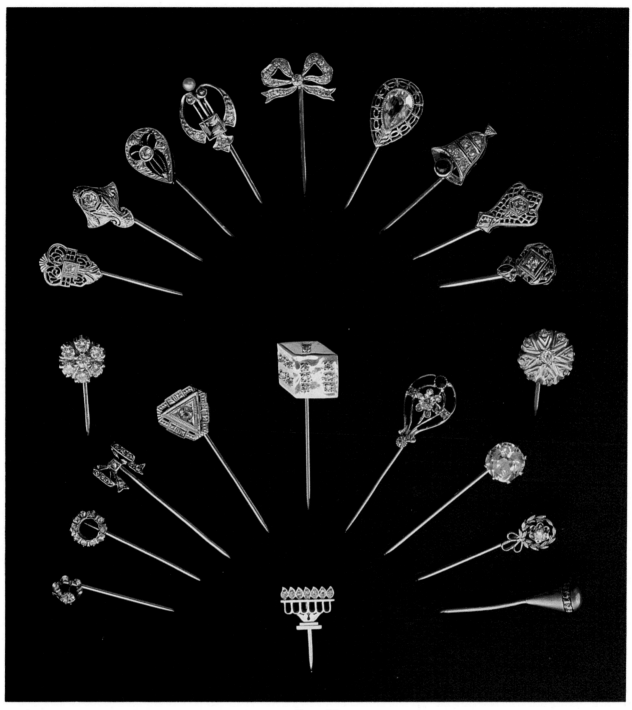

PLATE 20

TRIANGLE MOTIF • White gold pin and mount set with a single 3mm brilliant cut diamond, pin is marked "A/S-18K" with an illegible benchmark, Edwardian era. $125.00–175.00.

DIE MOTIF • Yellow gold pin and mount of a die set with eleven 2mm brilliant cut diamonds, Art Deco era. $200.00–300.00.

DIAMONDS • Yellow gold pin and mount set with one 4mm, one 3mm, and two 2mm single-cut diamonds and a 3mm garnet, Art Deco era. $125.00–175.00.

IMITATION DIAMOND • Yellow gold pin and Tiffany type mount set with a single 8mm faux diamond, Art Deco era. $75.00–100.00.

WREATH MOTIF • Rose gold pin with a white and rose gold mount set with a single 2mm brilliant cut diamond, pin is marked "10K," Edwardian era. $125.00–175.00.

SCARF PIN • Yellow gold pin and teardrop mount ringed with six 12mm rose-cut diamonds, early Victorian era. $75.00–100.00.

CENTERED AT BOTTOM

MENORAH MOTIF • Platinum pin and mount of a menorah with the flames of each of the seven candles set with a 2mm rose-cut diamond, late Victorian era. $250.00–350.00.

DOGS

It is little wonder that man's oldest and most faithful friend in the animal world should hold such a dominating influence in his works of art. Replicas of practically every breed of dog, from a treasured hunting companion to a toy terrier household pet, has been used for decades as the themes of paintings and motifs for various jewelry creations including stickpins.

Like horseshoes, hearts, and wishbones, the dog was so often featured that they are among the stickpins most commonly found by collectors today. Some of the finer pieces, however, are quite rare, especially the painted miniatures signed by the artists. The works of J.W. Bailey, William Essex, and William B. Ford are much sought after collectibles. Some of these were painted on porcelain, but they may also be found in reverse intaglio paintings under English crystal with ivory or pearl backgrounds.

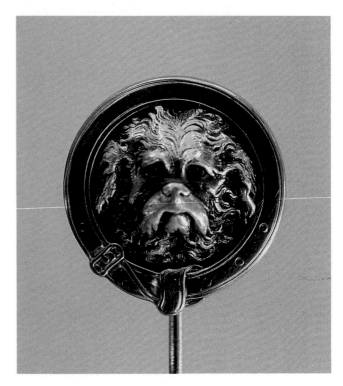

PEKINGESE • *Yellow gold pin and mount with a dog collar framing a silver Peke's face in relief, Art Nouveau era. $300.00–400.00.*

PLATE 21

TOP ARCH *(left to right)*

SEAL • Yellow gold pin with a gold chain dangling the three-dimensional figure of a pointer dog standing on a gold base. The underside of the base is an intaglio seal of another pointer carved in carnelian, mid-Victorian era. $200.00–350.00.

SPANIEL • Yellow gold pin and mount of a dog's head set with five seed pearls (plus one missing) in his collar and two ruby eyes, late Victorian era. $45.00–75.00.

ENGLISH CRYSTAL MOTIF • Yellow gold pin and mount framing a reverse intaglio painting of a pointer dog against a mother-of-pearl background, mount is marked "14K," late Victorian era. $200.00–300.00.

GREYHOUND • Yellow gold pin with gold profile of a dog with five 2mm rose-cut diamonds set in his collar and a mine-cut ruby in his mouth, pin is marked "750," mid-Victorian era. $200.00–300.00.

WELSH TERRIER • Yellow gold pin and mount framing a hand painted dog on porcelain, reverse is marked "G.H. Double Shear," signed and dated by the artist "Vinton P. Brese 1919," circa 1919. $300.00–400.00.

LABRADOR RETRIEVER • Yellow gold pin with gold profile of a dog with twelve 2mm rose-cut diamonds set in collar, mid-Victorian era. $200.00–300.00.

ENGLISH CRYSTAL MOTIF • Yellow gold pin and mount framing a reverse full view, intaglio painting of a Boston terrier, mount is marked "14K," late Victorian era. $250.00–350.00.

IRISH SETTER • Yellow gold pin and profile of a setter with a ruby eye superimposed upon a hunting horn, late Victorian era. $75.00–125.00.

ENGLISH SETTER • Yellow gold pin and mount with a three-dimensional figure of a setter on point, late Victorian era. $150.00–250.00.

CENTERED BETWEEN ARCHES

FRENCH POODLE • Silver pin and mount with three-dimensional figure of a poodle with a dinner pail in its mouth and chained with a padlock and a key, Edwardian era. $45.00–75.00.

BOTTOM ARCH *(left to right)*

BOXER'S HEAD • Yellow gold pin and three-dimensional mount of a carved tigereye boxer's head with a milk glass eye, Edwardian era. $100.00–150.00.

STARVED HOUND • Silver on copper pin and mount in the full body figure of a sad looking hound, Art Deco era. $25.00–45.00.

IRISH SETTER • Yellow gold pin and mount shaped like a setter's face with cabochon ruby eyes, Edwardian era. $75.00–125.00.

SPRINGER SPANIEL • Yellow gold pin mounted with a three-dimensional likeness of a spaniel's head in carved ivory, late Victorian era. $175.00–250.00.

LABRADOR RETRIEVER • Yellow gold pin and mount with a three-dimensional likeness of a Lab's head in carved amethyst, Edwardian era. $200.00–300.00.

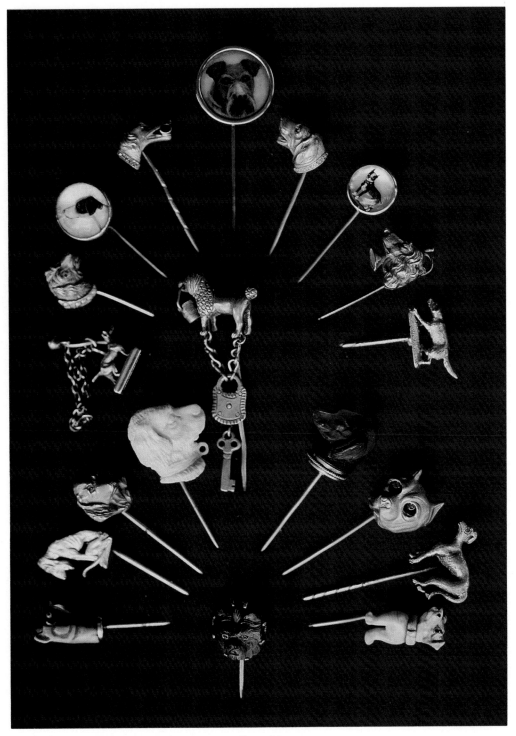

PLATE 21

BULLDOG • Yellow gold pin and mount in the likeness of a bulldog's head inset with spring mounted, crystal eyes made to shimmer, Art Deco era. $20.00–35.00.

GREYHOUND • Yellow gold pin and three-dimensional figure of a greyhound with ruby eyes, Edwardian era. $150.00–250.00.

TERRIER • Gold-plated pin and full front view of a terrier carved in ivory, Edwardian era. $50.00–100.00.

CENTERED AT BOTTOM

POMERANIAN • Yellow gold pin and mount with the face of a pomeranian exquisitely carved in tigereye and set with ruby eyes, Edwardian era. $175.00–250.00.

EGYPTIAN

The world has long been fascinated by the architecture and art works of the Egyptian civilization that existed some forty-five centuries before the birth of Christ. This is often exemplified in the jewelry reproductions of treasures found in the ancient tombs of the pharaohs.

Even from the early Georgian era, travelers from many nations visited the region of the Nile and the Valley of the Kings to view the awe-inspiring wonders from the early dynasties. Many returned to their homes with souvenirs that were later fashioned into jewelry items of all descriptions.

Among the popular motifs used in creating stickpins were mounted carvings of the sacred scarab, the symbol of Re, the Egyptian sun god. While many of these were trinkets sold to the tourists or reproductions cut from all types of stone, a few were authentic antiquities found in excavations. These, of course, are more valuable and highly collectible.

TUTANKHAMEN • *Brass pin and mount shaped in the likeness of King Tut, a ruler of Egypt during its most magnificent period of history, probably Art Deco era. $25.00–45.00.*

PLATE 22

FIRST ARCH (*left to right*)

SCARAB • Yellow gold pin and oval mount holding the likeness of a beetle carved in a cabochon carnelian with the figure of a man carved on the reverse, the mount is marked "S14C" (Strobell & Crane, Inc., Denmark, N.J.), circa 1909. $45.00–75.00.

SCARAB • Yellow gold pin and oval mount holding the likeness of a beetle carved in a cabochon piece of lapis lazuli with hieroglyphics cut on the reverse. The stone is quite old and is possibly a true relic retrieved by an early tourist. The stickpin came from the Gillette Family Estate (Gillette Razors), late Victorian era. $75.00–100.00.

SCARAB • Silver pin and gold-plated oval mount holding the likeness of a beetle carved in turquoise showing traces of matrix. The stickpin is very old and has been crudely repaired, it is possibly a true relic, Art Nouveau era. $25.00–45.00.

SCARAB • Silver pin and mount holding the likeness of a beetle carved from very old stone with a falcon carved on the reverse. It has been coated with a protective lacquer and could very well be an excavated piece set in an unusual, early Victorian mount. $75.00–100.00.

SCARAB • Silver pin and oval mount holding the likeness of a beetle etched in a piece of green glass, Art Deco era. $25.00–45.00.

SCARAB • Yellow gold pin and oval mount set with a very old turquoise carving of a beetle with hieroglyphics cut into the reverse, mount is marked "10K SN" (Sansbury & Nellis, Newark, New Jersey). The stickpin came from the Weldon Talley Estate, Terre Haute, Indiana, circa 1904. $45.00–75.00.

SCARAB • Yellow gold pin and oval mount set with the likeness of a beetle carved in a cabochon carnelian with a kneeling ancient Egyptian on reverse, pin is marked "14K," late Victorian era. $45.00–75.00.

SECOND ARCH (*left to right*)

FALCONS • Yellow gold pin and mount shaped in the likeness of a pair of falcons set with a seed pearl and a 2½mm mine-cut sapphire, reverse of mount is marked "14K," late Victorian era. $100.00–150.00.

LADY'S HEAD • Gold plate on copper pin and mount of an Egyptian lady's head set with red and clear single-cut imitation stones, Art Nouveau era. $25.00–45.00.

EGYPTIAN GOD • Yellow gold pin and mount shaped in the likeness of an ancient god with the winged body of a lion and the head of a woman and set with a 2½mm mine-cut garnet, late Victorian era. $45.00–75.00.

THIRD ARCH (*left to right*)

PHARAOH'S HEAD • Silver pin and copper mount shaped in the likeness of an ancient Egyptian king inlaid with dark red enamel, Art Nouveau era. $25.00–45.00.

PHARAOH • Yellow gold pin and mount shaped in the front image of a pharaoh inlaid in blue, white, and brown enamel, reverse is marked "14," late Victorian era. $75.00–100.00.

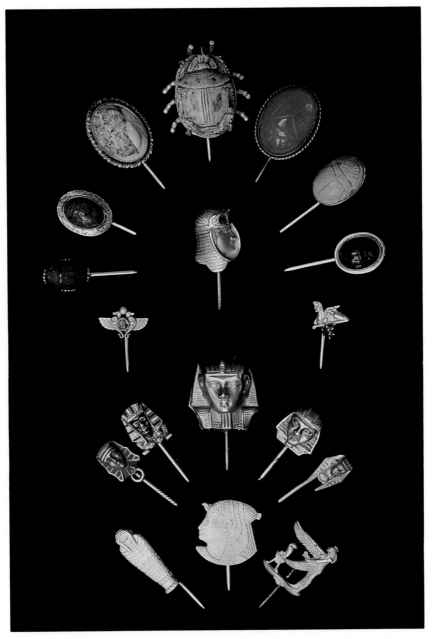

PLATE 22

TUTANKHAMEN • Brass pin and mount shaped in the likeness of Egypt's most recognized pharaoh, Art Nouveau era. (Note: This is the same pin shown in the lead photo at the beginning of this category.) $25.00–45.00.

TUTANKHAMEN • Silver pin and mount shaped in the likeness of King Tut set with red, white, blue, and green inlaid enamel, reverse is marked "STERLING," Art Nouveau era. $45.00–75.00.

PHARAOH • Gold-plated pin and mount shaped in the likeness of an Egyptian ruler, Art Nouveau era. $15.00–25.00.

BOTTOM ARCH

MUMMY CASE • Gilded pin and mount shaped in the likeness of a mummy case, reverse is marked "BEN-AMUN - copyright," late Victorian era. $20.00–35.00.

HATSHEPSUT • Gold-filled pin and mount shaped in the likeness of Egypt's greatest queen in left profile, Art Nouveau era. $45.00–75.00.

EGYPTIAN GOD • Silver pin and gold-filled mount in the likeness of Horus, the Egyptian god with the body of a man and the head of a falcon, as he stands before the symbol of Re, the sun god depicted in the form of Uraeus the cobra, Art Nouveau era. $15.00–25.00.

EMERALDS AND GREEN STONES

Legend has it that the emerald originated with the Greek goddess, Venus, and it is known that this beautiful gem was mined in Egypt more than 2,000 years before the birth of Christ. It is the birthstone for the month of May and is among the most prized and costly of all gemstones.

Only the very finest emeralds are free of inclusions and those are so rare they are often priceless. Therefore, the majority of true emeralds we stickpin collectors see will have a few flaws.

In a way, this is a help to those of us who are strictly amateurs when appraising the quality of gems. We should approach with caution those expensive pins with flawless green stones touted to be "perfect" gems.

Another thing we should remember is that the emerald may easily be confused with the peridot. Normally, this lesser expensive stone will show more of a yellowish cast.

PERIDOTS AND DIAMOND • *Yellow gold pin and round mount set with ten 2mm single-cut peridots surrounding a 2mm single cut diamond, Art Deco era. $75.00–$100.00.*

PLATE 23

UPPER ARCH *(left to right)*

EMERALD • Yellow gold pin and mount set with a 4.5mm brilliant cut emerald, pin is marked "N-14K" (Wm. F. Newhall, Lynn, Mass.), circa 1907. $125.00–175.00.

IMITATION EMERALDS • Gold-plated pin and mount with a circular piece of green glass cut and set to resemble channel set emeralds, Art Deco era. $10.00–25.00.

IMITATION EMERALD • Gold-plated pin and mount set with an oval piece of green glass, Art Deco era. $10.00–25.00.

PERIDOT • Yellow gold pin and mount set with a hexagon-cut peridot and a single seed pearl, pin marked "10K," Art Deco era. $50.00–75.00.

PERIDOT • Yellow gold-plated pin and rose gold on silver-plated mount set with a French-cut peridot, Edwardian era. $45.00–60.00.

PERIDOT • Yellow gold pin and gold filigree mount set with an oval-cut peridot, pin marked "S.M. & S. - 10K" (Scofield, Melcher, and Scofield, Plainville, Mass.), circa 1904. $50.00–75.00.

PERIDOT • Gold-plated pin and mount set with a French-cut peridot, Edwardian era. $45.00–60.00.

IMITATION EMERALD • Gold-plated pin and mount set with a faux emerald and a single mine-cut rhinestone, Art Nouveau era. $10.00–25.00.

SYNTHETIC EMERALD • Gold-plated pin and mount set with a French-cut synthetic emerald, pin hallmarked "R" (C. Ray Randall & Co., North Attleboro, Mass.), circa 1909. $20.00–40.00.

SHOWN AT LEFT AND RIGHT

EMERALD • Yellow gold pin and white gold mount set with a 2½mm single-cut emerald (the stone is chipped), mount is marked on reverse "9K GOLD TOP," late Victorian era. $25.00–45.00.

EMERALD • White gold pin and filigree mount set with a square cut emerald, pin marked "10K," late Victorian era. $60.00–100.00.

SECOND ARCH *(left to right)*

DOUBLETS • Rose gold pin and shamrock-shaped mount set with three green rose-cut doublets, Edwardian era. $20.00–40.00.

EMERALD AND DIAMOND • Yellow gold pin and mount set with a 5mm brilliant cut emerald and four 2mm rose-cut diamonds, late Victorian era. $125.00–175.00.

FAUX EMERALD AND DIAMOND • Yellow gold pin and mount set with a round faux emerald with a concaved table and a 2mm rose-cut diamond, Edwardian era. $20.00–40.00.

EMERALDS • Yellow gold pin and railroad spike motif mount channel set with 10 graduated square-cut emeralds, hallmarks on pin illegible. (Note: This stickpin reputedly came from the John D. Rockefeller Estate.) $200.00–300.00.

EMERALD • Yellow gold pin and mount with a brilliant cut emerald, Art Deco era. $100.00–175.00.

EMERALD • Yellow gold pin and Tiffany type mount set with a 6mm brilliant cut emerald, Edwardian era. $150.00–200.00.

EMERALD • Yellow gold pin and claw motif mount set with a square-cut emerald, Art Deco era. $125.00–175.00.

PLATE 23

BOTTOM ARCH *(left to right)*

IMITATION EMERALD • Gold-plated pin and white metal mount set with teardrop-shaped faux emerald and six rhinestones, Art Nouveau era. $10.00–20.00.

IMITATION EMERALD AND DIAMOND • White metal pin and mount set with a green glass, emerald-cut stone and a 2mm brilliant cut faux diamond, Art Deco era. $15.00–25.00.

PERIDOT • Yellow gold pin and Tiffany type mount set with a 4mm European-cut peridot, Art Nouveau era. $35.00–50.00.

EVENTS AND ORGANIZATIONS

In the mid-Victorian era, it became quite popular to proudly wear pieces of jewelry displaying the crests and logos of various organizations or to commemorate special events. This fad continued throughout the remainder of the stickpin era and carried over to our present day use of tie-tacks and lapel pins.

Many fraternal organizations were founded in the years following the Civil War, and some of the stickpins worn by the members were made of precious metals and set with jewels. This, of course, must also be considered in determining the pin's present value.

Most of those commemorating events were like advertising pins – cheaply made, giveaway items. However, these often bore the date the event took place thereby confirming their historical era. Regardless of their material value, such dated pieces are highly collectible today.

MILITARY CREST • *Silver pin and brass mounted inlaid blue enameled crest lettered "THE ROYAL BRITISH LEGION," Art Nouveau era. $15.00 – 25.00.*

PLATE 24

TOP ROW *(left to right)*

N.E.A. MEETING • Silver pin and box-shaped mount with mountain scene in relief lettered "PIKE'S PEAK N.E.A." (National Educational Association) "DENVER 1895," reverse of mount stamped "Sterling," circa 1895. $15.00 – 25.00.

N.E.A. MEETING • Gold plate on copper pin and mount cast in relief and lettered "NATIONAL EDUCATIONAL ASSOCIATION – UTAH 1913," maker's name on reverse of mount "The Whitehead & Hoag Co. Newark, N.J.," circa 1913. $15.00 – 25.00.

BANKER'S MEETING • Gold-filled pin and red, white, and blue inlaid enameled mount lettered "DELEGATE ABA AMERICAN BANKERS ASSN. CHICAGO 1909," maker's name on reverse of mount "Dieges & Clust 23 Johnst. N.Y.," circa 1909. $20.00 – 35.00.

N.E.A. MEETING • Silver pin and mount bearing image of Fort Snelling and lettered "NATIONAL EDUCATION ASSOCIATION ST. PAUL, MINN. JULY 4-11, 1914 ASSOCIATE," circa 1914. $15.00 – 25.00.

N.E.A. MEETING • Silver pin and mount depicting sailing vessel on ocean, lettered "1905 NATIONAL EDUCATIONAL ASSOCIATION," reverse of mount marked "The Whitehead & Hoag Co., Newark, N.J.," circa 1905. $15.00 – 25.00.

SECOND ROW *(left to right)*

I.S.M.A. MEETING • Yellow gold pin with white and red inlaid enameled mount depicting red devil, lettered "I.S.M.A. WEST BADEN – FRENCH LICK 1905," (West Baden and French Lick were southern Indiana resort/convention centers at turn of the century), maker's name on reverse of mount is "The Whitehead & Hoag Co. Newark, N.J." with hallmark of International Jewelry Workers of America, circa 1905. $20.00 – 35.00.

POSTAL WORKERS ASSOCIATION • Silver pin and mount lettered "NATIONAL ASSOCIATION OF LETTER CARRIERS" around the image of a hand holding an envelope marked "U.S.A.," reverse of mount is marked "FECHHIMER UNIFORMS," probably Art Nouveau era. $15.00 – 25.00.

N.E.A. MEETING • Gold-filled pin and mount shaped like a running bison, lettered "N.E.A. '96," maker's name on reverse of mount is "HEINZ BROS. BUFFALO, N.Y.," circa 1896. $20.00 – 35.00.

A B I • Gold-filled pin and mount shaped like an arrowhead with raised left profile of an Indian chieftain and the entwined letters "A B I" (American Bankers Institute) and the word "INDIANA," maker's name on reverse of mount is "BASTIAN BROS. CO. ROCHESTER, N.Y.," late Victorian era. $20.00 – 35.00.

S H S • Yellow gold pin and red and white inlaid enameled diamond-shaped mount with the entwined script letters "S H S" and "94," (probably a high school class of 1894 pin), reverse of mount hallmarked "LE," circa 1894. $20.00 – 35.00.

THIRD ROW *(left to right)*

COLUMBIAN EXPO • Gold-plated pin and coin replica mount of thin stamped metal with the head of Columbus, lettering reads "WORLDS COLUMBIAN EXPOSITION 1893," circa 1893. $10.00 – 20.00.

O.A.W.C. • Silver pin and heart-shaped mount with the hand engraved letters "O.A.W.C. 1892," circa 1892. $10.00 – 20.00.

MASONIC • Gold-filled pin and inlaid red and white enameled mount with crossed shovel and pick and a shield lettered "S T K S H T W S" surrounded by the lettering "INDIANAPOLIS CHAPTER No. 5 JUNE 11, 1909," reverse of mount marked "BUSCHMANN, GRIFFEY CO. INDIANAPOLIS, IND.," circa 1909. $15.00 – 25.00.

PLATE 24

HIGH SCHOOL CLASS PIN • Yellow gold pin with the date "'94" forming the mount which is engraved "T H H S," (Terre Haute High School 1894). $20.00–35.00.

AX HEAD • Brass pin and mount shaped like an ax head, engraved "McINTOSH 1905," circa 1905. $15.00–25.00.

FOURTH ROW *(left to right)*

VETERANS REUNION • Gold-filled pin and mount inlaid with red, white, and blue enamel with wreath and crossed sabers, entwined letters "SV," and "1883 L.S.A.," circa 1883. $15.00–25.00.

RED DEVIL • Gold-plated pin and triangular mount inlaid with white, blue, red, and yellow enamel, shows red devil with pitchfork standing over fire, probably Art Nouveau era. $15.00–25.00.

MUSIC FESTIVAL • Silver pin and disc-shaped mount with raised lyre and lettered "LIEDERKRANZ HEGENSBERG 1872," circa 1872. $15.00–25.00.

A B I • Yellow gold pin and mount inlaid with red, white, and blue enamel and shaped like head of Indian chieftain with entwined letters "A B I" (American Bankers Institute) and "1911 INDIANAPOLIS,"

reverse of mount marked "Whitehead & Hoag Co. Newark, N.J.," circa 1911. $35.00–50.00.

MASONIC • Gold-filled pin and mount inlaid with red and white enamel with crossed pick and shovel and shield lettered "S T K S H T W S," surrounded by "INDIANAPOLIS CHAPTER No. 5," reverse marked "Bastian Bros. Co. Roch. N.Y.," circa 1909. $10.00–20.00.

FIFTH ROW *(left to right)*

CENTENNIAL PIN • Gold-plated pin with eagle and replica coin mount showing image of log cabin, lettered "JEFFERSON COUNTY CENTENNIAL STEUBENVILLE, O. 1897," reverse shows head of Liberty, circa 1897. $15.00–25.00.

WORLD'S FAIR PIN • Gold-plated pin with an eagle and replica coin mount showing The Hall of Science, lettered "A CENTURY OF PROGRESS 1933," reverse has micro lettering of the Lord's Prayer, circa 1933. $25.00–35.00.

CARNIVAL PIN • Gold-plated pin with an eagle and replica coin mount lettered on a banner around a parade float "CARNIVAL JUBILEE 1898 TERRE HAUTE," reverse shows the image of a court jester, circa 1898. $15.00–25.00.

PLATE 25

FIRST ROW (*left to right*)

MASONIC • Brass pin and rose gold engraved mount shaped like Mason's trowel with ivory handle, late Victorian era. $45.00–75.00.

32ND DEGREE MASON • Gold-plated pin and double eagle mount with inlaid dark blue enameled triangle lettered "32," late Victorian era. $15.00–25.00.

SHRINE • Silver plate on copper pin, mount shaped like a Shriner's face with a red and white inlaid enameled fez, late Victorian era. $25.00–35.00.

32ND DEGREE MASON • Heavy gold pin and double eagle mount with triangle lettered "32," reverse is engraved "C. HARRIS" and "LCIOTO," late Victorian era. $200.00–300.00.

SHRINE • Yellow gold pin and ivory inlaid mount of The Order of the Mystic Shrine, mount marked "14K" and hallmarked with letter "R" above scimitar (Rinker Bros., Newark, N.J.), circa 1898. $45.00–75.00.

32ND DEGREE MASON • Gold-plated pin and triangle-shaped mount engraved "32," late Victorian era. $15.00–25.00.

MASONIC • Gold-plated pin and Rose Croix-shaped mount inlaid with white, red, and green champlevé enamel, late Victorian era. $45.00–75.00.

SECOND ROW (*left to right*)

MASONIC • Gold-plated pin and oval mount hand engraved with the square, dividers, and "G" of a Master Mason and the numbers "573," late Victorian era. $15.00–20.00.

ODD FELLOWS • Yellow gold pin and yellow, green, and rose gold oval mount with the three rings and letters "F L T" of the Odd Fellows Lodge, pin is marked "R & F" (Riley & French, North Attleboro, Mass.), circa 1898. $25.00–45.00.

M W A PIN • Gold-plated pin and oval mount with red and green champlevé enamel crest lettered "M W A" (Modern Woodmen of America), reverse of mount marked with back-to-back letters "F–F" (Frank Flynn Co., Providence, R.I.), circa 1912. $25.00–45.00.

MASONIC AUXILIARY • Yellow gold pin and Maltese cross mount inlaid with red, black, and white enamel, lettered "INHOC SIGNO VINCES" and "WOODLAWN LADIES' TEMPLAR CLUB," reverse marked "C.A. Winship Chicago," circa 1922. $25.00–45.00.

SHRINE • Gold plate on silver pin with an inlaid red, green, and blue enameled mount shaped in the crest of the Order of the Mystic Shrine depicting two cobras and a scarab, reverse of mount marked "800," late Victorian era. $25.00–45.00.

MASONIC • Yellow gold pin and oval mount engraved with dividers, square, and "G" of Master Mason, reverse stamped "S & C" (Strobell & Crane, Inc., Newark, N.J.), circa 1909. $25.00–45.00.

MASONIC • Yellow gold pin and shield-shaped mount inlaid with black, blue, and red enamel with the double eagle, Jerusalem cross, and triangle marked "32," reverse is stamped "Robbins Attleboro," circa 1892. $35.00–50.00.

THIRD ROW (*left to right*)

ELKS LODGE • Yellow gold pin and mount with the elk head and clock on a blue and white inlaid enameled emblem of Benevolent & Protective Order of Elks, elk's head set with two cabochon ruby eyes, late Victorian era. $125.00–200.00.

K OF C LODGE • Gold washed pin and Maltese cross-shaped mount inlaid with red, white, and blue inlaid enameled emblem of the Knights of Columbus, late Victorian era. $5.00–15.00.

F C B • Gold plate on copper pin and mount of the yellow, red, and blue champlevé enameled emblem of the Knights of Pythias, late Victorian era. $25.00–35.00.

MOOSE LODGE • Yellow gold pin and mount shaped in the emblem of Loyal Order of Moose, set with 21 pearls (one pearl is missing), reverse stamped "14K" with arrow hallmark, late Victorian era. $125.00–200.00.

ELKS LODGE • Yellow gold pin and mount shaped in left profile of an elk with ruby eye and 2mm mine-cut diamond set between antlers, reverse of mount hallmarked with rose for "Henry Freund & Bros., New York, N.Y.," circa 1896. $60.00–100.00.

MOOSE LODGE • Yellow gold pin and white gold mount shaped in left profile of moose with ruby eye and 2mm single cut diamond set between the antlers, late Victorian era. $60.00–100.00.

ELKS LODGE • Gold-filled pin and mount shaped in the left profile of a bugling elk with the raised letters "BPOE" on its neck, late Victorian era. $45.00–75.00.

FOURTH ROW (*left to right*)

XI PSI PHI • Yellow gold pin and oval mount with raised Greek letters of college fraternity, reverse engraved "FRANK B. BENESH" and stamped "14K," probably late Victorian era. $45.00–75.00.

SIGMA PI • Gold-filled pin and diamond-shaped mount inlaid with black enamel and the gold Greek letters of a college fraternity pledge pin, probably late Victorian era. $15.00–25.00.

SIGMA NU • Gold-filled pin and oval mount with raised Greek letters of college fraternity, probably late Victorian era. $25.00–45.00.

W C T U • Yellow gold pin and mother-of-pearl mount shaped like a ribbon tied in a bow and incised with the letters "W C T U" (Woman's Christian Temperance Union), circa 1883. $25.00–45.00.

SIGMA CHI • Gold plate on copper pin and mount shaped in the crest of a college fraternity, reverse is marked "D.L. Auld Co." (Columbus, Ohio), circa 1909. $15.00–25.00.

Y M C A • Gold-plated pin and mount with raised inverted triangle marked "SPIRIT MIND BODY" (emblem of the Young Men's Christian Association), probably Art Deco era. $15.00–25.00.

DELTA SIGMA DELTA • Silver pin and copper mount shaped like flint spearhead with raised silver Greek letters of college fraternity, reverse marked "Brochon, Chicago," circa 1922. $25.00–45.00.

FIFTH ROW (*left to right*)

RUSSIAN ORGANIZATION • Gold-plated pin and wreath-shaped mount with a hammer and sickle and raised red and white bassetaille enamel star and rampant lion, pin is lettered "SVAZARM," probably Art Nouveau era. $25.00–45.00.

G V • Silver pin and gold-plated square mount with blue and white inlaid enamel and a star with the entwined letters "G V," source unknown, probably late Victorian era. $25.00–45.00.

SPECIAL EVENT • Steel pin and enameled button type mount showing the colored likeness of a 19th century fireman, lettering reads "FIREMAN'S CELEBRATION," reverse of mount is marked "Hastian Bros., Chester, N.Y.," late Victorian era. $20.00–35.00.

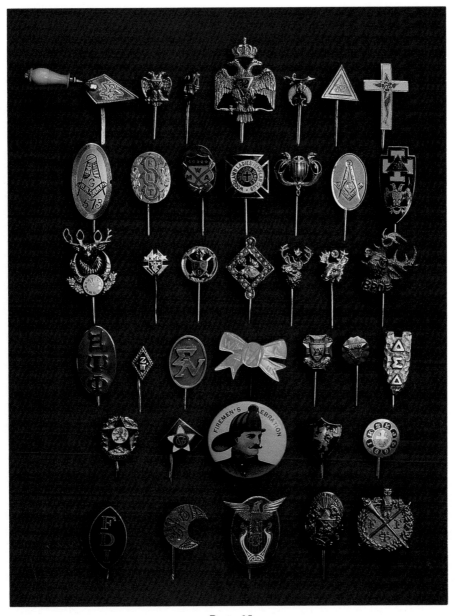

PLATE 25

BRITISH ORGANIZATION • Silver pin and blue inlaid enameled shield-shaped mount with a rampant lion and the letters "DNT," probably late Victorian era. $25.00–45.00.

K S K J • Gold-plated pin and yellow gold disc-shaped mount with blue and white inlaid enamel and gold cross with lettering "K S K J 1894," reverse of mount marked "14K," circa 1894. $25.00–45.00.

SIXTH ROW *(left to right)*

DANISH • Silver pin and marquise-shaped mount with blue inlaid enamel and the silver letters "F D I," reverse of mount marked "Made in Denmark," probably late Victorian era. $25.00–45.00.

D OF R • Gold-filled pin and crescent-shaped mount hand engraved "D of R" (Daughters of Rebecca), probably late Victorian era. $15.00–25.00.

MUSIC FESTIVAL • Silver pin and gold-filled oval mount with blue and white inlaid enamel showing gold eagle perched atop a music lyre and letters "C C C," reverse is stamped "The Whitehead & Hoag Co. Newark, N.J." and hallmark of International Jewelry Workers of America, circa 1905. $25.00–45.00.

CONVENTION PIN • Silver pin and copper oval-shaped mount with a raised fraternity crest and lettering "4TH BIENNIAL CONVENTION 1914," reverse is stamped "The H & S Co. Phila.," circa 1914. $25.00–45.00.

F F T S • Gold-plated pin and thin stamped metal mount in the shape of a wreath with crossed pike and torch topped by a perched owl and lettered "F F" and the entwined letters "T S," probably Art Nouveau era. $5.00–15.00.

FACES

When studying the wide variety of motifs found in stickpin designs, one quickly comes to realize that the human face is undoubtedly the most often used. In almost every material from gold to granite and in every era from the ancient rulers of the Nile Valley to Presidents of the United States, the facial features of famous people have been portrayed in these jewelry creations.

In fact, we find that faces of individuals are the dominating themes in 18 of the more than 50 categories of stickpins covered in this book. From cameos and coins to political pins and portraits, the countenances of men and women of every race, historical era, and station in society are displayed here.

ORVILLE WRIGHT • *Gold plate on copper pin and mount in the likeness of the man who successfully flew the first airplane. His goggles are set with single-cut rhinestones for lenses, Art Nouveau era. $15.00–25.00.*

PLATE 26

FIRST ROW *(left to right)*

WARRIOR AND LADY • Gold-filled pin and mount shaped in the likenesses of an ancient warrior and his lady in right profile, late Victorian era. $20.00–35.00.

SLAVE • Gold-filled pin and mount shaped in the left profile likeness of a slave with a bandanna around her head, mid-Victorian era. $25.00–45.00.

ORIENTAL • Gold-plated pin and mount shaped in the likeness of an Oriental man, late Victorian era. $25.00–45.00.

CABIN BOY • Gold-filled pin and mount shaped in the likeness of a young British sailor, late Victorian era. $25.00–45.00.

WARRIOR • Gold plate on copper pin and mount shaped in the left profile of an ancient warrior wearing a helmet and with three seed pearls set in his collar, late Victorian era. $30.00–50.00.

SECOND ROW *(left to right)*

LINCOLN • Gold-plated pin and mount shaped in the right profile of Abraham Lincoln, circa 1863. $10.00–15.00.

QUAKER • Silver pin and oval mount bearing the likeness of a Quaker man, late Victorian era. $10.00–15.00.

LADY • Gold plate on copper pin and mount with the gold right profile of a Victorian lady against a green inlaid enamel background, late Victorian era. $25.00–45.00.

NAPOLEON • Copper pin and silver plate on brass round mount with the raised likeness of Napoleon Bonaparte in left profile facing his crest, a crown over the letter "N," mount marked with the artist's initials, "E.D.," mid-Victorian era. $25.00–45.00.

ROYALTY • Gold-filled pin and mount shaped in the likeness of a queen, late Victorian era. $20.00–35.00.

THIRD ROW *(left to right)*

SHAKESPHERE • Silver pin and oval mount bearing the raised likeness of the famous "Bard of the Avon," reverse is marked "Sterling," late Victorian era. $25.00–45.00.

NOMAD • Silver pin and mount bearing the raised likeness of a Middle Eastern tribesman, reverse shows a box-shaped hallmark, late Victorian era. $25.00–45.00.

GEORGE WASHINGTON • Silver plate on copper pin and oval mount bearing the likeness of the first President of the United States, late Victorian era. $25.00–45.00.

DANISH LADY • Silver pin and round mount bearing the image of a Danish woman working with a spindle, late Victorian era. $25.00–45.00.

WILLIAM I • Silver pin and oval mount bearing the likeness of the first Kaiser of Germany, reverse is marked "CHILDS CHICAGO," Edwardian era. $20.00–35.00.

PLATE 26

FOURTH ROW *(left to right)*

TURKISH MAN • Yellow gold pin and mount with the face of a Middle Eastern man carved from red jasper and wearing a baroque pearl turban set with a 2mm single-cut diamond, pin is marked "14K," late Victorian era. $200.00–300.00.

HINDU MAN • Silver pin and mount shaped like the face of a Hindu wearing an inlaid enameled turban (enamel is chipped), late Victorian era. $10.00–15.00.

SHEIK • Yellow gold pin and mount on a Middle Eastern ruler wearing a red, blue, and gold enameled turban set with a 2mm mine-cut diamond, reverse of mount is marked "14K," late Victorian era. (Note: This pin is unique in that the man's face and the turban are two separate pieces held together with a screw on the reverse.) $1,000.00–1,500.00.

ARABIC MAN • Gold plate on silver pin and mount shaped in the likeness of a Middle Eastern man, pin is marked "STERLING," late Victorian era. $15.00–20.00.

PERSIAN MAN • Yellow gold pin and mount shaped in the likeness of a Middle Eastern man, reverse is marked "14K," late Victorian era. $45.00–75.00.

FIFTH ROW *(left to right)*

ORIENTAL MAN • Gold plate on copper pin and mount shaped in the likeness of an Oriental man with a mustache and single-cut ruby eyes, late Victorian era. $35.00–60.00.

ORIENTAL MAN • Yellow gold pin and mount shaped in the left profile of an Oriental man with a mine-cut diamond eye and an inlaid blue enamel queue forming the script letter "ELI," reverse is marked "14K," late Victorian era. $100.00–150.00.

FISH AND WILDLIFE

In the late Victorian era and the years leading into the turn of the century, much interest was given to the critters of the marine and animal kingdoms. Naturally, this manifested itself in the motifs used in the jewelry of the time. The trend carried over into the Art Nouveau era, and continues on even today. Influenced by the vast population of sport fishermen and hunters and our current awareness of the ecology and environment, the popularity of this motif is still in vogue.

The wide variety of animal species involved innately provided an endless choice of subjects for the artisans who created the old stickpins shown in this category. A few are of modern vintage, but the majority are antiques, and while mostly inexpensive, some are comparatively rare and quite valuable. The reverse intaglio paintings under English crystal (circa 1870-1920), for example, are commanding very high prices on today's market.

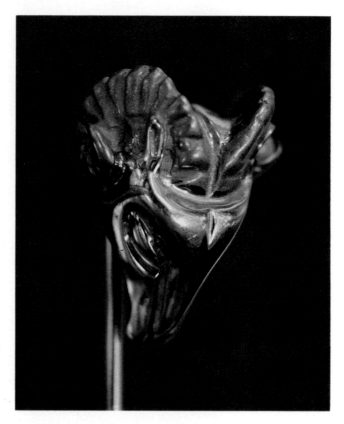

BIGHORN SHEEP • *Yellow gold pin and mount shaped like the head of a Rocky Mountain bighorn sheep, pin is marked "14K," Art Nouveau era. $75.00–125.00.*

PLATE 27

FIRST ROW *(left to right)*

ELEPHANT • Yellow gold pin and mount shaped in the three-dimensional likeness of a walking elephant, Art Deco era. $150.00–250.00.

RACCOON • Gold plate on silver pin and mount shaped in the likeness of a raccoon, reverse is marked in large raised numbers "1915" and "W & H Co." (Whiteman & Hogue Co., Providence, R.I.), circa 1915. $25.00–45.00.

DEER • Silver pin and mount in the shape of a walking fawn pavé set with marcasite, reverse is marked "STERLING," Art Nouveau era. $50.00–75.00.

RAMBOUILLET • Gold-filled pin and mount shaped like the head of a domestic range sheep, Art Nouveau era. $25.00–45.00.

HYENA • Yellow gold pin and flat topped mount with the three-dimensional likeness of a hyena, Art Deco era. $150.00–250.00.

SECOND ROW *(left to right)*

BAT • Gold-filled pin and mount shaped in the likeness of a flying bat, late Victorian era. $40.00–60.00.

KANGAROO • Gold washed pin and mount in three-dimensional likeness of a kangaroo, souvenir pin. $3.00–8.00.

FOX • Gold-filled pin and round mount holding the reverse intaglio painting on English crystal of a fox's head, mid-Victorian era. $200.00–300.00.

KOALA • Yellow gold pin and mount in the shape of a koala climbing a tree, reverse of mount is marked "Stokes, Melb." (Australia), late Victorian era. $15.00–25.00.

DOLPHIN • Yellow gold pin and three-dimensional mount of a jumping dolphin, modern. $75.00–100.00.

THIRD ROW *(left to right)*

CARIBOU • Silver pin and oval mount with a basse-taille enameled arctic scene depicting caribou running across snow with aurora borealis in background, reverse stamped "925S NE" and hand engraved with initial "A," late Victorian era. $50.00–95.00.

KOALA • Gold-plated pin and mount in the three-dimensional likeness of a koala bear holding a black opal doublet, modern. $15.00–25.00.

CAMEL • Gold plate on copper pin and mount in three-dimensional likeness of a walking camel (badly worn finish), Art Deco era. $5.00–10.00.

BEAR • Gold-plated pin and mount in the likeness of a rearing grizzly bear, Art Deco era. $5.00–10.00.

BUFFALO • Gold-filled on copper pin and mount in the likeness of an American bison with a cabochon ruby eye, Art Deco era. $25.00–45.00.

PLATE 28

THIRD ARCH *(left to right)*

LILY • Yellow gold pin and flower mount set with a pearl and a 2mm single-cut rose quartz, late Victorian era. $25.00–45.00.

LEAF MOTIF • Yellow gold pin and leaf mount set with three seed pearls, pin marked "10K" and "W" (Werner Bros., New York, N.Y.), circa 1922. $30.00–50.00.

FORGET-ME-NOT • Yellow gold pin and flower mount with inlaid enamel, set with 13 seed pearls, late Victorian era. $60.00–80.00.

SWEET PEA • Yellow gold pin and flower mount with inlaid enamel and a single 2mm mine-cut diamond, late Victorian era. $150.00–250.00.

ANEMONE • Yellow gold pin and mount set with six petals of baroque pearls and a single 2mm mine-cut rose quartz, late Victorian era. $75.00–100.00.

LEAVES MOTIF • Gold-filled pin and mount set with 13 seed pearls, (two need replacing), Edwardian era. $15.00–25.00.

FOUR LEAF CLOVER • Yellow gold pin and mount set with four seed pearls and single 2mm opal, late Victorian era. $30.00–50.00.

BOTTOM ARCH *(left to right)*

IRIS • Yellow gold pin and flower mount set with a single pearl, late Victorian era. $100.00–125.00.

LILY-OF-THE-NILE • Yellow gold pin and inlaid enameled mount set with a baroque pearl, pin is marked "14K," late Victorian era. $75.00–100.00.

LILY • Yellow gold pin and flower mount with five channel set graduated seed pearls and a 2mm single-cut diamond, late Victorian era. $75.00–100.00.

HEARTS AND HANDS

No two motifs are more fitted to share the same category than hearts and hands. Both have been liberally displayed in paintings, sculptures, and jewelry designs for centuries, and the popular use of both reached their peaks during the Victorian eras.

More than anything else, the heart has always been the symbol of everlasting love and devotion, but most of all it is the personification of life itself. It is often said that gestures made with the human hands openly manifest the feelings of the heart. There are even those who claim that the positions of the hands substitute for uttered words of Christ and the Apostles in Leonardo da Vinci's painting, *The Last Supper.*

In more recent times, the extended finger of a hand has been used to call attention to advertised items or, when pressed to the lips, it is a request for silence or secrecy.

HEART • *Yellow gold pin and heart-shaped mount set with a hand painting of flowers on porcelain, reverse of mount is hand engraved with the script initials "A.A.," late Victorian era.* $75.00–125.00.

PLATE 29

UPPER ARCH *(left to right)*

DOUBLE HEART • Gold-plated pin and mount set with alternating blue and white enameled beads, late Victorian era. $10.00–20.00.

HEART AND LEAF MOTIF • Gold-plated pin and mount set with one seed pearl and two garnets, late Victorian era. $25.00–35.00.

HEART AND GARNETS • Yellow gold pin and mount set with eighteen 2mm cabochon garnets, late Victorian era. $40.00–60.00.

HEART AND FLOWER • Yellow gold pin and mount set with a single-cut garnet, pin is hallmarked "C.T." (Cheever, Tweedy Co., North Attleboro, Mass.), circa 1915. $25.00–35.00.

LARGE HEART • Gilded metal pin and mount set with a large artificial pearl heart, modern. $2.00–5.00.

HEART AND ARROW • Rose gold pin and mount set with 10 seed pearls, one 2mm mine-cut garnet, and one 2mm mine-cut diamond, pin is marked "14K," late Victorian era. $75.00–125.00.

HEART • Gold-plated pin and mount set with a blue frosted glass heart, Art Deco era. $15.00–25.00.

HEART • Silver pin with gold plate on silver mount set with 11 graduated seed pearls, Edwardian era. $25.00–45.00.

HEART AND SAPPHIRE • White gold pin and mount set with a star sapphire, pin marked "14K," late Victorian era. $60.00–80.00.

SECOND ARCH *(left to right)*

HEART • Gold plate on silver pin and mount set with a single pearl, reverse of mount is marked "STER.," Edwardian era. $30.00–50.00.

HAND AND SHIELD • Gold-plated pin and mount with hand holding mother-of-pearl shield mounted with yellow gold letter "K," Art Deco era. $10.00–20.00.

LOCKET • Gold-plated pin and mount with brushed enameled heart-shaped locket, Art Nouveau era. $15.00–25.00.

THIRD ARCH *(left to right)*

DOUBLE HEART • Gold plate on silver pin and mount, reverse of mount is marked "STAR" and a hallmark, Edwardian era. $20.00–30.00.

HEART • Silver pin and mount set with a single-cut rhinestone, Edwardian era. $10.00–20.00.

HAND • Yellow gold pin and mount of a hand holding a mine-cut rose quartz stone, pin is marked "10K," late Victorian era. $25.00–50.00.

HAND • Gilded metal pin and mount of a hand holding an artificial single-cut garnet, Edwardian era. $10.00–20.00.

HAND • Gold-plated pin and mount with a coral colored Bakelite hand holding a single-cut rhinestone, Art Nouveau era. $40.00–60.00.

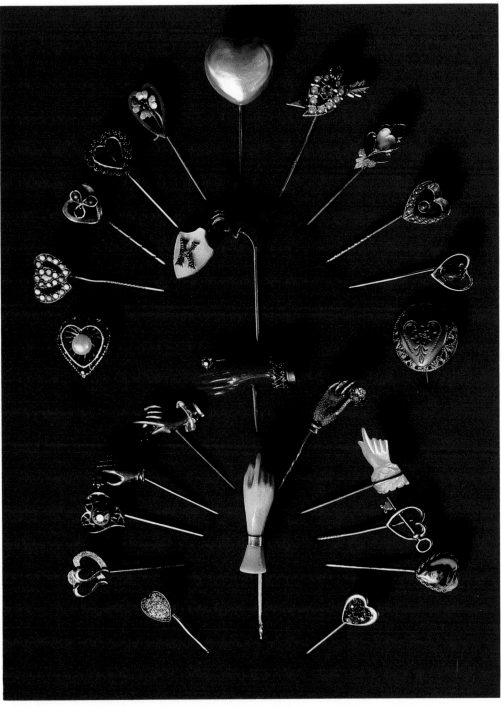

PLATE 29

HAND • Gold-filled pin and hand-shaped mount holding a mine-cut rhinestone, Edwardian era. $25.00–45.00.

HAND • Gold-plated pin and yellow gold mount with a mother-of-pearl hand with index finger extended, late Victorian era. $25.00–45.00.

HEART AND KEY • Gold-plated pin mounted with a silver heart crossed with a key, Art Deco era. $15.00–25.00.

HEART AND FACE • Gold washed pin and mount set with a painting on porcelain of a youth wearing an Alpine hat, mid-Victorian era. $30.00–75.00.

BOTTOM ARCH (*left to right*)

HEART • Yellow gold pin and mount set with a goldstone heart, late Victorian era. $25.00–45.00.

HAND • Gold-filled pin and mount with a carved ivory hand with index finger extended, late Victorian era. $50.00–75.00.

HEART • Gold-plated pin and heart-shaped mount set with nine mine-cut rhinestones, Edwardian era. $15.00–25.00.

HORSESHOES, HORSES, AND THE HUNT

Prior to the invention of the automobile, the horse was the primary means of land transportation, so it was only natural that horses and horse related motifs were used extensively in the era when wearing stickpins was at its peak. This was also during the years when such pins graced the scarfs and ascots of those who patronized the famous race tracks and participated in the sport of fox hunting.

Today, horseshoes, horses, hunting horns, and foxes are among the most common designs found by collectors of antique stickpins. As may be expected, the quality in materials used and craftsmanship exhibited in these pins will range from just mediocre to the very finest.

Many of the stickpins in this category are among the most desirable pieces a collector can own.

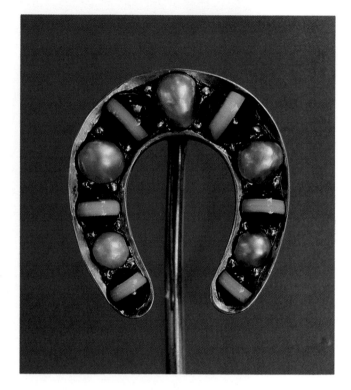

HORSESHOE • *Yellow gold pin and horseshoe-shaped mount with alternate settings of five pearls and six cabochons of black and white banded onyx, late Victorian era. $100.00–150.00.*

PLATE 30

UPPER ARCH *(left to right)*

HORSESHOE • Yellow gold pin and horseshoe mount with three green enameled four-leaf clovers and three seed pearls, pin marked "14K" and a hallmark, late Victorian era. $60.00–80.00.

HORSESHOE • Yellow gold pin and horseshoe mount with eleven 2mm mine-cut, blue spinel stones, late Victorian era. $100.00–150.00.

HORSESHOE • Yellow gold pin and horseshoe mount with fifteen 2mm mine-cut gems – seven rubies and eight diamonds, late Victorian era. $250.00–350.00.

HORSESHOE • Silver plate on brass pin and horseshoe mount crossed by a running fox, late Victorian era. $25.00–50.00.

HORSESHOE • Gold-filled on copper pin and horseshoe mount set with 11 pearls, late Victorian era. $100.00–175.00.

HORSESHOE • Yellow gold pin and dangling horseshoe mount set with braided horse hair, late Victorian era. $100.00–150.00.

HORSESHOE • Yellow gold pin and horseshoe mount set with eight 2mm mine-cut diamonds, pin marked "14K," late Victorian era. $250.00–350.00.

HORSESHOE • Yellow gold pin and horseshoe mount set with seventeen 2mm rose-cut garnets (one stone is missing), late Victorian era. $40.00–60.00.

HORSESHOE • Yellow gold pin and horseshoe mount set with 10 pearls and crossed with a riding crop, pin is marked "9 ct," late Victorian era. $75.00–125.00.

SHOWN AT LEFT AND RIGHT

TINY HORSESHOE • Yellow gold pin and horseshoe mount set with nine pearls and crossed by a gold snake with a single-cut emerald eye, late Victorian era. $50.00–75.00.

HORSESHOE • Yellow gold pin and horseshoe mount set with nine pearls surrounding one 2mm mine-cut ruby, pin is marked "9K," late Victorian era. $100.00–150.00.

LOWER ARCH *(left to right)*

HORSESHOE • Gold-plated pin and horseshoe mount with twisted gold rope coiled around a 4mm synthetic ruby, late Victorian era. $25.00–50.00.

HORSESHOE • Yellow gold pin and horseshoe mount set with 11 graduated rhinestones surrounding a yellow gold horse head, pin is marked "14K" with hallmark, late Victorian era. $50.00–75.00.

HORSESHOE • Silver plate on copper pin and gunmetal-blue silver horseshoe mount with copper nail heads showing, late Victorian era. $30.00–50.00.

HORSESHOE • Silver pin and horseshoe mount with silver horse head pavé set with rhinestones and a synthetic ruby eye, mount is marked "Sterling," Edwardian era. $35.00–75.00.

LARGE HORSESHOE • Vermeil pin and horseshoe-shaped mount, late Victorian era. $50.00–75.00.

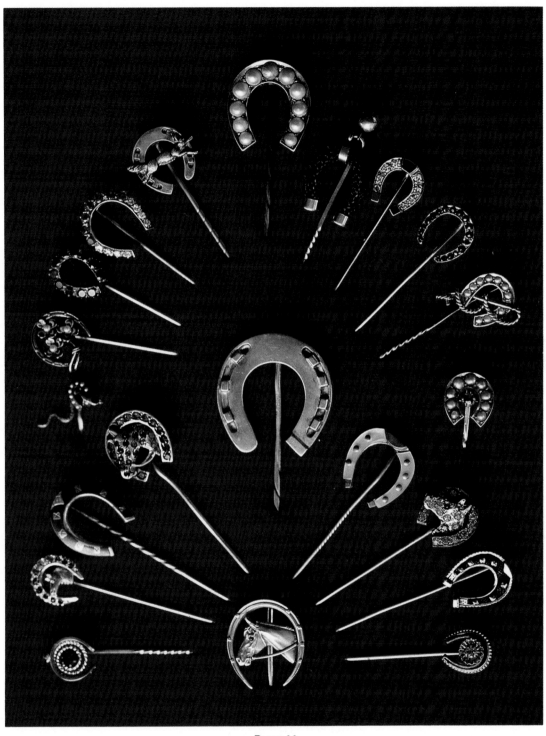

PLATE 30

HORSESHOE • Gold-plated pin and horseshoe mount set with mother-of-pearl overlay and brass nail heads, late Victorian era. $20.00–35.00.

HORSESHOE • Silver pin and horseshoe mount with horse's head pavé set with rhinestones and a garnet eye, mount is marked "Sterling," Edwardian era. $35.00–75.00.

HORSESHOE • Yellow gold pin and horseshoe mount channel set with braided horse hair and gold nail heads, late Victorian era. $125.00–200.00.

HORSESHOE • Gold-plated pin and horseshoe mount inlaid with black enamel around a flower set with a 3mm mine-cut rhinestone, late Victorian era. $20.00–35.00.

CENTERED AT BOTTOM

HORSESHOE • Yellow gold pin and horseshoe mount surrounding a gold horse's head set with a ruby eye, pin is marked "14K," late Victorian era. $75.00–125.00.

PLATE 31

UPPER ARCH *(left to right)*

STIRRUP WITH STRAP • Yellow gold pin and stirrup mount with a white gold strap and buckle, late Victorian era. $40.00–60.00.

ENGLISH CRYSTAL • Silver pin and mount with a reverse intaglio painting of two horses and hunters going over jumps, late Victorian era. $75.00–125.00.

TWO STIRRUPS • Yellow gold pin mounted with one white gold and one yellow gold stirrup, pin is marked "14K" and hallmarked with a crescent and arrow (Whiteside & Blank, Newark, N.J.), circa 1904. $75.00–100.00.

HORSE'S HEAD • Gold-plated pin and an enameled horse head mount, late Victorian era. $15.00–25.00.

HORSE'S HEAD • Yellow gold pin and mount with an inlaid enamel painting of a horse's head, late Victorian era. $100.00–150.00.

HORSE'S HEAD • White metal pin mounted with an enameled horse's head on brass, Edwardian era. $25.00–45.00.

FOX'S HEAD • White metal pin with copper mount of fox's face peering from the brush, late Victorian era. $25.00–45.00.

ENGLISH CRYSTAL • Gold-plated pin and mount with reverse intaglio painting of horse's head, late Victorian era. $50.00–75.00.

HORSE'S HEAD • Gold-plated pin and horse head mount with a mine-cut rhinestone set in its bridle, Edwardian era. $25.00–45.00.

SHOWN AT LEFT AND RIGHT

HUNTER'S HORN • Brass pin and mount, Edwardian era. $15.00–25.00.

HUNTER'S HORN • Brass pin and mount, Edwardian era. $15.00–25.00.

LOWER ARCH *(left to right)*

HORSESHOE • Rose gold pin and horseshoe-shaped mount crossed with a gold riding crop dangling a 3mm rhinestone, late Victorian era. $40.00–60.00.

STIRRUP • Gold-plated pin and mount crossed with a riding crop, late Victorian era. $25.00–45.00.

FOX'S HEAD • Yellow gold pin and translucent enamel over yellow gold fox head mount, pin is marked "18K," late Victorian era. $150.00–250.00.

HORSESHOE • Yellow gold pin and horseshoe mount set with 11 pearls, late Victorian era. $100.00–150.00.

RUNNING HORSE • Yellow gold pin and mount holding a carved ivory horse, late Victorian era. $50.00–75.00.

HORSESHOE • Gold-plated pin mounted with a riding crop and horseshoe overlaid with mother-of-pearl and set with a 2mm rose-cut amethyst, late Victorian era. $30.00–50.00.

FOX'S HEAD • Yellow gold pin and fox head mount set with ruby eyes, reverse of mount is marked "14K," late Victorian era. $100.00–125.00.

RIDING CROP • Gold-plated pin and riding crop mount, Edwardian era. $15.00–25.00.

SMALL HORSESHOE • Gold-plated pin and horseshoe mount crossed by a running horse, late Victorian era. $25.00–45.00.

CENTERED AT BOTTOM

RUNNING FOX • Yellow gold pin and mount of a running fox pavé set with ten 2mm rose-cut diamonds and a ruby eye, late Victorian era. $100.00–200.00.

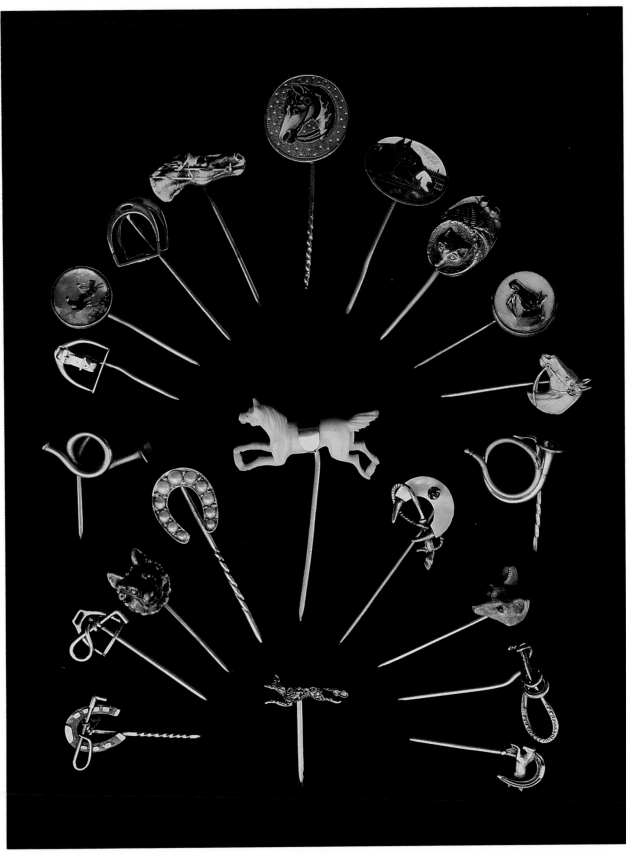

PLATE 31

INSECTS

Among the oldest, and certainly most numerous and prolific life forms on this planet are those found in the world of insects. So vast is the diversification in species and classes of insects throughout the world that it is quite doubtful even half have ever been recorded.

Far back in the history of ancient Egypt, the scarab, or dung beetle, was known and considered sacred. Even in those long ago eras, likenesses of this insect were reproduced in gold and carved gemstones to be used as personal adornments. It is not surprising then that jewelers in the heyday of the stickpin should often use replicas of all types of insects as motifs for their creations.

Many examples were crudely made and little more than pure junk, but some, fabricated from precious metals and mounted with exquisite gems, are highly valued and desired pieces.

BUTTERFLY • *Yellow gold pin and round mount with a preserved butterfly housed under English crystal against the background of an authentic, blue butterfly wing, reverse of mount is marked "14K," late Victorian era. $75.00–100.00.*

PLATE 32

FIRST ROW *(left to right)*

BEE • Yellow gold pin and mount shaped in the likeness of a flying bee set with a 4mm pearl and eight seed pearls, Art Nouveau era. $60.00–80.00.

BEETLE • Gold-plated pin and mount holding a preserved green bodied beetle, late Victorian era. $25.00–45.00.

CRICKET • Gold tone pin and brass mount in the likeness of a cricket with a long oval body of faceted amber-colored glass, Art Deco era. $15.00–25.00.

BEETLE • Gold-plated pin and mount holding the green, red, and gold enameled metal image of a beetle, Art Deco era. $15.00–25.00.

BUTTERFLY • Yellow gold pin and mount shaped in the likeness of a small butterfly and set with four cabochon opal wings, Art Deco era. $50.00–75.00.

SECOND ROW *(left to right)*

BUTTERFLY • Gold-plated pin and mount shaped in the likeness of a small butterfly with gold filigree wings, late Victorian era. $25.00–45.00.

FLY • Yellow gold pin and mount shaped in the likeness of a common housefly with four seed pearls set in the wings, pin is marked "10K," late Victorian era. $50.00–75.00.

BEETLE • Gold-filled pin and mount shaped in the likeness of a flying beetle with a long oval amethyst set in its body, late Victorian era. $20.00–35.00.

FLY • Yellow gold pin and mount shaped in the likeness of a common housefly set with a 2mm rose-cut ruby, eight rose-cut diamonds in white gold wings, and a tubular hexagon ruby body, late Victorian era. $150.00–175.00.

BUTTERFLY • Yellow gold pin and mount shaped in the likeness of a small butterfly set with three 2mm mine-cut diamonds, late Victorian era. $60.00–80.00.

THIRD ROW *(left to right)*

BEETLE • Brass pin and mount shaped in the likeness of a small beetle and set with an oval cabochon piece of turquoise, Art Deco era. $15.00–25.00.

DRAGONFLY • Gold-filled pin and round mount set with the hand-painted likeness of a dragonfly on a pearl enameled background, late Victorian era. $25.00–45.00.

HORSEFLY • Silver pin and oval-shaped silver mount with the raised likeness of a horsefly, Edwardian era. $25.00–45.00.

FLY • Yellow gold pin and oval mount framing the likeness of a common housefly made of ivory and black onyx with glass wings, Art Deco era. $150.00–200.00.

BEETLE • Gilded metal pin and mount shaped in the likeness of a flying beetle with filigree rings and set with a cabochon turquoise, Art Deco era. $15.00–25.00.

PLATE 32

FOURTH ROW *(left to right)*

BEE • Gold-plated pin and stamped copper mount in the shape of a bee on a flower blossom, Art Deco era. $15.00–25.00.

GRASSHOPPER • Gold-plated pin and mount shaped in the likeness of a grasshopper in green and white champlevé enamel, reverse is stamped "WHITEHEAD & HOAG CO. NEWARK, N.J.," circa 1922. $10.00–20.00.

BEETLE • Yellow gold pin and mount shaped in the likeness of a beetle and set with a body of two cabochon amethysts and one cabochon citrine stone, late Victorian era. $300.00–375.00.

BUTTERFLY • Gold-plated pin and mount shaped in the likeness of a butterfly in red, blue, and green champlevé enamel, Art Deco era. $15.00–25.00.

FLY • Gold-plated pin and mount shaped in the likeness of a small fly with inlaid enameled wings and body, late Victorian era. $15.00–25.00.

CENTERED AT BOTTOM

BUTTERFLY • Gold plate on silver pin and mount shaped in the likeness of a butterfly with yellow and black inlaid enameled wings, reverse of mount is marked "OX-ST" (Oxford Jewelry Corp., Philadelphia, Penn.), Art Deco era. $15.00–25.00.

INTAGLIOS

Intaglios are actually the opposite of cameos. While the cameo figure is a raised or relief carving, the intaglio is cut down into the medium used in a piece of jewelry. There is nothing new about this art form, for the practice was known and used more than 5,000 years before the coming of Christ.

Some of the finest examples of intaglio works come from Italy, and many of the motifs used related to ancient warriors, or to the gods of Roman and Greek mythology.

Practically every material and gemstone has been used as a medium for cutting intaglios that were then set in all types of jewelry from bracelets and brooches to rings and stickpins. Their popularity peaked in the mid-Victorian era and strongly came into vogue again during the Art Nouveau years.

APHRODITE AND EROS • *Yellow gold pin and oval mount holding a flat piece of amber-tinted crystal with the likenesses of these two Greek deities, known as Venus and Cupid in Roman mythology, cut into the reverse, mid-Victorian era. $75.00–125.00.*

PLATE 33

TOP ROW (*left to right*)

APHRODITE • Yellow gold pin and oval mount set with an amethyst intaglio in the likeness of the Greek goddess, mid-Victorian era. $35.00–50.00.

GRECIAN LADY • Gold plate on copper pin and mount holding an oval amethyst intaglio in the likeness of a Greek lady, late Victorian era. $25.00–45.00.

ROMAN WARRIOR • Yellow gold pin and round mount set with carnelian intaglio in the likeness of an ancient Roman soldier, late Victorian era. $75.00–100.00.

HORSE • Yellow gold pin and mount set with black onyx intaglio in the likeness of a horse's head, reverse of mount is marked "14K," Art Nouveau era. $75.00–125.00.

ARISTOTLE • Yellow gold pin and oval mount set with an amethyst intaglio in the likeness of the young Greek pupil of Plato, late Victorian era. $35.00–50.00.

SECOND ROW (*left to right*)

WARRIOR • Yellow gold pin and oval mount set with an amethyst intaglio in the likeness of an ancient helmeted warrior, late Victorian era. (Note: This stickpin is one of five that was reputedly owned by Sam Starr, husband of the notorious outlaw queen, Belle Starr.) $35.00–50.00.

MERCURY • Yellow gold pin and mount set with bloodstone intaglio in the likeness of the Roman god with his winged helmet, pin is marked "10K," late Victorian era. $60.00–80.00.

ROMAN WARRIOR • Yellow gold pin and mount set with a faceted amethyst intaglio in the likeness of a helmeted Roman soldier, late Victorian era. $150.00–200.00.

STAG • Yellow gold pin and rectangular mount set with carnelian intaglio in the likeness of a running stag leaping over a fence, Art Nouveau era. $60.00–80.00.

DIANA • Gold-plated pin and oval mount set with a clear red stone intaglio in the likeness of the Roman goddess of the moon, late Victorian era. $35.00–50.00.

THIRD ROW (*left to right*)

ROMAN WARRIOR • Gold-plated pin and oval mount set with in opaque green stone intaglio in the likeness of a helmeted Roman soldier, late Victorian era. $35.00–50.00.

PLATO • Yellow gold pin and oval mount set with a carnelian stone intaglio in the likeness of the Greek philosopher, late Victorian era. $60.0–80.00.

HEBE • Yellow gold pin and oval mount in twisted rope design set with a cabochon agate intaglio in the likeness of the goddess Hebe, late Victorian era. $75.00–100.00.

PLATE 33

DIANA • Gold-plated pin and oval mount set with a clear red stone intaglio in the likeness of the Roman goddess, late Victorian era. $40.00–60.00.

ARISTOTLE • Gold-plated pin and shield-shaped mount set with an opaque green stone intaglio in the likeness of the young Greek pupil of Plato, late Victorian era. $25.00–45.00.

FOURTH ROW *(left to right)*

GREEK WARRIOR • Yellow gold pin and mount set with carnelian intaglio in the likeness of a young Greek soldier, late Victorian era. $45.00–75.00.

APHRODITE • White gold pin and keystone-shaped mount set with citrine intaglio in the likeness of the Greek goddess, late Victorian era. $45.00–75.00.

MAN-IN-THE-MOON • Yellow gold pin and round mount set with mother-of-pearl intaglio in the likeness of a crescent with the face of a man looking at a star, Art Nouveau era. $45.00–75.00.

GREEK WARRIOR • Gold-plated pin and oval mount set with an opaque green stone intaglio in the likeness of young Greek soldier, late Victorian era. $35.00–50.00.

GREECIAN LADY • Gold-plated pin and mount set with imitation topaz intaglio in the likeness of a Greek woman, late Victorian era. $25.00–45.00.

LIONS AND TIGERS

Lions and tigers are the largest members of the Felidae family, and since biblical times have been respected for their power, courage, and unchallenged royalty above all others in the animal kingdom.

The lion, especially, has had such a profound influence on mankind that these traits have caused his image to be used symbolically on the flags and crests of nations and ruling clans throughout the world. Even the touchmarks and trademarks of artists and industries have used the likeness of the lion as a sign of quality and excellence in their products. It is not surprising then, that the big cats are frequently found in the motifs that were used in designing antique stickpins.

LION • *Yellow gold pin and round mount framing the ¹¹/₁₆″ diameter micromosaic likeness of a lion's head in right profile, mid-Victorian era. $350.00–400.00.*

PLATE 34

FIRST ROW *(left to right)*

RAMPANT LION • Yellow gold pin and mount in the shape of a rampant lion with a 2mm mine-cut ruby in its paw, mid-Victorian era. $75.00–100.00.

LION OF ST. MARK • Yellow gold pin and three-dimensional mount in the shape of a winged lion with a halo and front foot resting on a book of scriptures. This is the symbol of Mark the Evangelist and is also the emblem of the city of Venice. The pin is marked "750," mid-Victorian era. $100.00–125.00.

BRITISH LION • Yellow gold pin and mount in the shape of seated lion with a 2mm ruby eye and front paw resting on a globe which in this case is a 4mm brilliant cut diamond, mid-Victorian era. $300.00–350.00.

WALKING LION • Copper pin and a stamped copper mount shaped in the body of a walking lion, Art Deco era. $5.00–10.00.

LION OF ST. MARK • Yellow gold pin and mount of a winged lion with halo and front foot resting on a book of scriptures, pin is marked "750," mid-Victorian era. $50.00–75.00.

SECOND ROW *(left to right)*

LION'S HEAD • Gold-plated pin and stamped mount of a lion's face with a single-cut rhinestone in its mouth, Art Deco era. $15.00–25.00.

LION'S HEAD • Gold-filled pin and mount shaped like a lion's face with two cabochon ruby eyes and a 2mm single-cut diamond in its mouth, late Victorian era. $50.00–75.00.

LION'S HEAD • Yellow gold pin and mount shaped like lion's face with two cabochon ruby eyes and a 2mm mine-cut diamond in its mouth, pin is marked "18K," late Victorian era. $150.00–200.00.

LION'S HEAD • Gold-plated pin and mount shaped like a lion's face with a pearl in its mouth, late Victorian era. $15.00–25.00.

LYNX HEAD • Gold-plated pin and mount shaped in the likeness of a lynx's face with a 3mm mine-cut rhinestone in its mouth, late Victorian era. $25.00–35.00.

THIRD ROW *(left to right)*

LION'S HEAD • Gold-filled pin and mount shaped like a lion's face with a 2mm mine-cut imitation diamond in its mouth, late Victorian era. $15.00–25.00.

LION'S HEAD • Gold-plated pin and oval mount set with eight single-cut rhinestones framing the right profile of a lion with a red glass eye, Art Deco era. $25.00–50.00.

LION'S HEAD • Yellow gold pin and ivory mount carved in shape of a lion's head in left profile, late Victorian era. $50.00–100.00.

TIGER'S HEAD • Gold plate on copper pin and oval-shaped mount framing the enameled right profile of a tiger, late Victorian era. $35.00–50.00.

LIONESS • Silver pin and mount of a lioness attacking an oval cabochon of red glass, Art Deco era. $15.00–25.00.

PLATE 34

FOURTH ROW *(left to right)*

LION'S HEAD • Gilded pin and mount shaped like a lion's face with two red glass eyes and a 2mm single-cut rhinestone in its mouth, late Victorian era. $25.00–35.00.

TIGER'S HEAD • Yellow gold pin and inlaid translucent enameled mount shaped like a tiger's face with a 2mm mine-cut diamond in its mouth, reverse of mount is marked "14K," late Victorian era. $200.00–300.00.

LION'S HEAD • Yellow gold pin and round mount framing the ¹¹⁄₁₆" diameter micromosaic likeness of a lion's head in right profile, mid-Victorian era. (Note: This is the same pin shown in the lead photo of this category.) $350.00–400.00.

LION'S HEAD • Yellow gold pin and mount in the shape of a lion's face with two rose-cut ruby eyes and a pearl in its mouth, late Victorian era. $125.00–175.00.

LION'S HEAD • Gold-filled pin and mount shaped like a lion's face with a long oval cabochon imitation ruby set in its widely gaping jaws, Art Nouveau era. $25.00–45.00.

MEMORIAL AND HAIR

During both the middle and latter parts of the Georgian Era and all of the Victorian Era, it was not uncommon for a departed loved one to be publicly mourned for months or even years. Not only was black clothing worn, but this outward expression of bereavement was carried over into jewelry as well. Naturally, this included stickpins.

Quite often pieces of the deceased's hair were kept as a memorial. Sometimes, these were braided, woven, or coiled beneath a crystal or glass compartment on the pin so that a part of the beloved would always be near. Some of this memorial jewelry was marked with names, initials, and/or dates, and today, such stickpins are rare and very collectible.

Some jewelry pieces displaying human hair were also given by one lover to another as a token of fidelity.

PLAITED HAIR • *Yellow gold pin and black on gold inlaid enameled mount set with a round cabochon black and white-banded onyx crossed with inlaid gold lettering "IN MEMORY OF," plaited brown hair is displayed under crystal on reverse of mount, mid-Victorian era. $300.00–400.00.*

PLATE 35

FIRST ROW *(left to right)*

MOURNING PIN • White gold pin and yellow gold mount faced with a flower carved in jet with a black onyx bead, late Victorian era. $50.00–75.00.

MOURNING • Yellow gold pin and mount faced with a flower carved in jet with a 2½mm mine-cut diamond, late Victorian era. $100.00–150.00.

MOURNING PIN • Yellow gold pin and mount set with a cabochon of black and white banded onyx, mid-Victorian era. $75.00–100.00.

MOURNING PIN • Rose gold pin and mount shaped like a memorial wreath inlaid with pieces of black onyx and set with a single seed pearl, mid-Victorian era. $75.00–100.00.

MOURNING PIN • Yellow gold pin and gold mount shaped like three carved jet flowers each set with a seed pearl, mid-Victorian era. $100.00–150.00.

SECOND ROW *(left to right)*

MOURNING PIN • Yellow gold pin and square gold mount set with a piece of black onyx and a diamond chip, mid-Victorian era. $35.00–50.00.

MOURNING PIN • Yellow gold pin and diamond-shaped gold mount inlaid with a piece of black onyx set with a 3mm mine-cut diamond and surrounded by 34 seed pearls, mid-Victorian era. $100.00–125.00.

MOURNING PIN • Gold-plated pin and mount set with an oval cabochon of black and white banded onyx, late Victorian era. $50.00–75.00.

MOURNING PIN • Yellow gold pin and white gold kite-shaped mount inlaid with a piece of black onyx and set with a 2mm mine-cut diamond, pin is marked "14K," late Victorian era. $50.00–75.00.

MOURNING PIN • Silver pin and square mount inlaid with a piece of black onyx and set with two 2mm single-cut rhinestones, late Victorian era. $35.00–50.00.

THIRD ROW *(left to right)*

MOURNING PIN • Yellow gold pin and white gold hexagon-shaped mount inlaid with a piece of black onyx set with a 2mm single-cut diamond, pin is hallmarked "R&F" (Riley, French, & Heffron, North Attleboro, Mass.), circa 1909. $35.00–50.00.

MOURNING PIN • Rose gold pin and oval mount inlaid with black enamel, late Victorian era. $50.00–75.00.

MOURNING PIN • Yellow gold pin and round mount set with white onyx and topped with a gold wreath, a gold six-pointed star with black inlaid enamel, and set with a pearl, late Victorian era. $75.00–100.00.

MOURNING PIN • Yellow gold pin and white gold rectangular mount set with black onyx and topped with a Persian turquoise bead, late Victorian era. $50.00–75.00.

MOURNING PIN • White gold pin and mount inlaid with an oval piece of black onyx set with a 2mm mine-cut diamond, late Victorian era. $40.00–60.00.

PLATE 35

FOURTH ROW *(left to right)*

MOURNING PIN • Yellow gold pin and round gold mount set with black onyx and a seed pearl, late Victorian era. $60.00–80.00.

MOURNING PIN • Yellow gold pin with yellow and white gold marquise-shaped mount inlaid with black onyx, pin is marked "(G) 14K," late Victorian era. $40.00–60.00.

MOURNING PIN • Yellow gold scarf pin topped with a gold double ringed mount set with a bar of black onyx, late Victorian era. $60.00–80.00.

MOURNING PIN • White gold pin and oval mount set with black onyx and 2mm mine-cut diamond, late Victorian era. $50.00–75.00.

MOURNING PIN • White gold pin and mount finished in black enamel and set with a 2mm single-cut rhinestone, late Victorian era. $20.00–30.00.

FIFTH ROW *(left to right)*

MOURNING PIN • Gold-plated pin and open round mount featuring a basse-taille enameled Maltese cross set with a black onyx bead, pin is marked "H A & CO" (Horton, Angell & Co., Attleboro, Mass.), circa 1870. $40.00–60.00.

MOURNING PIN • White gold pin and mount inlaid with black enamel and set with a single pearl, late Victorian era. $35.00–50.00.

MOURNING PIN SET • Yellow gold pin topped with star engraved jet ball and chained to a yellow gold guard pin, late Victorian era. $50.00–75.00.

MOURNING PIN • Yellow gold pin and marquise-shaped gold mount inlaid with a piece of black onyx set with a 2mm rose-cut diamond, pin is marked "14K," late Victorian era. $40.00–60.00.

MOURNING PIN • Yellow gold pin and round gold mount circled with inlaid black enamel in the Greek key design and topped with a gold star set with a pearl, late Victorian era. $75.00–100.00.

PLATE 36

FIRST ROW *(left to right)*

PLAITED HAIR • Yellow gold wavy stemmed pin with green and white inlaid enameled gold mount, plaited gray hair displayed under crystal in the marquise-shaped mounting, late Georgian era. $400.00–500.00.

LADY'S PORTRAIT • Rose gold pin and rose gold oval crystal faced mount, left portrait of lady painted on ivory and framed by seed pearls set on an opalescent background surrounded by pearl stars, reverse of gold mount engraved with initials "GW," mid-Georgian era. (Note: This stickpin is the oldest in this collection, probably dating back to the middle part of the 18th century. Due to its age, some of the seed pearls and stars have dissolved over the years, but it is a very rare stickpin indeed.) $500.00–600.00.

PLAITED HAIR • Yellow gold pin and gold oval crystal-faced mount with gold script initials "E L" against plaited brown hair background, Georgian era. $200.00–300.00.

MOURNING PIN • Yellow gold wavy-stemmed pin and gold marquise-shaped mount. A sepia painting on ivory of a Grecian lady standing beside a tomb is displayed under crystal. The lettered border of painting reads "7 MAY 1787 AE 55 HON. H. WOOD. OB." Lettering on tomb reads "HEAVEN HAS RELIEVED AFFLICTION." This is a very rare pin, circa 1787. $600.00–900.00.

COILED HAIR • Yellow gold wavy-stemmed pin hinged to back of red inlaid enameled gold mount. Coils of brown hair displayed under crystal face of marquise-shaped mounting, late Georgian era. $400.00–500.00.

SECOND ROW *(left to right)*

MOURNING PIN • Gold-filled pin and oval mount finished in black and white enamel. Hair compartment on reverse of mount is empty, early Victorian era. $50.00–75.00.

PLAITED HAIR • Yellow gold pin and drum-shaped concave faced mount set with replica of a broken shield with black enameled "H," lettering around side of drum reads "IN MEMORIAM DH DIED NOV. 12 AD 1887." Brown hair displayed under glass on reverse of mount, circa 1887. $300.00–400.00.

PLAITED HAIR • Yellow gold pin and black on gold inlaid enameled mount set with a round cabochon of black and white banded onyx crossed with inlaid gold lettering "IN MEMORY OF," plaited brown hair is displayed under crystal on mount, mid-Victorian era. (Note: This is the same stickpin shown in the lead photo of this category.) $300.00–400.00.

RELIGIOUS RELIC • Yellow gold pin and round gold mount faced with a raised Maltese cross set with 16 Persian turquoise beads, a piece of tightly woven cloth is encased on the reverse of the mount, early Victorian era. $150.00–200.00.

PLAITED HAIR • Yellow gold pin and black enameled gold mount lettered in gold "IN MEMORY OF" and set with a round cabochon of black and white banded onyx with a six-point gold star set with a single pearl, brown hair is displayed in compartment on reverse of mount, mid-Victorian era. $250.00–350.00.

THIRD ROW *(left to right)*

PLAITED HAIR • Gold-plated pin and black inlaid enameled gold plated square mount set with a 2mm single-cut rhinestone in each corner, brown hair is displayed under round glass dome, mid-Victorian era. $100.00–150.00.

PLAITED HAIR • Yellow gold pin and inlaid black enameled gold mount lettered "IN MEMORY OF," brown hair displayed under glass, reverse of pin engraved "CHARLOTTE HOOK OBt 14 SEPt 1828 AE 40," circa 1828. $200.00–300.00.

PLAITED HAIR • Yellow gold pin and safety chained mount featuring an inlaid black enameled gold serpent with agate eyes coiled around an oval glass-covered compartment holding brown hair, reverse is engraved "L. F. AUGt 13th 1852," circa 1852. $350.00–400.00.

DISSOLVED HAIR • Yellow gold pin and hinged gold mounting. Under crystal face, brown hair on pearl background creates scene of two fishermen standing under a tree beside a stream, reverse is engraved "A. R. BROOKS," mid-Victorian era. $275.00–325.00.

COILED HAIR • Yellow gold pin and inlaid black enameled gold mount set with four 2mm rose-cut diamonds and a 4mm mine-cut diamond. Brown hair displayed under glass in compartment on reverse, late Victorian era. $150.00–200.00.

FOURTH ROW *(left to right)*

PLAITED HAIR • Yellow gold pin and inlaid black enameled gold rectangular mount, brown hair displayed under beveled glass, late Victorian era. $150.00–200.00.

PLAITED HAIR • Yellow gold pin and circular mount with brown hair displayed under crystal face, late Victorian era. $225.00–275.00.

PLAITED HAIR • Yellow gold pin and rectangular gold mount edged with 24 matched pearls, two shades of hair are displayed under crystal face, late Victorian era. $250.00–350.00.

PLAITED HAIR • Yellow gold wavy stemmed pin and round gold mount set with thirteen 2½mm mine-cut diamonds, brown hair is displayed under crystal face, reverse is engraved with initials "E.M.," Georgian era. $450.00–550.00.

PLAITED HAIR • Yellow gold pin and arched rectangular gold mount, brown hair displayed under crystal face, late Victorian era. $200.00–300.00.

SHOWN AT BOTTOM *(left to right)*

BRAIDED HAIR • Yellow gold pin with brown hair braided around gold anchor-shaped mount, late Victorian era. $100.00–150.00.

BRAIDED HAIR • Yellow gold pin with brown braided hair around a gold mount shaped like a music lyre, late Victorian era. $250.00–300.00.

PLATE 36

MICROMOSAICS, MOSAICS, AND PIETRA DURA

Mosaics are artistic works created by fitting together pieces of stone or glass of various colors to form designs that are held in place with cement. The art dates back to the ancient Assyrians and Egyptians, but was better known and extensively used by the Romans.

While mosaics were used in decorating the walls and floors of palaces and churches, the art was refined in Florence and Venice where tiny pieces were employed in creating jewelry. Special examples of the Florentine works, known as "pietra dura," are usually found in floral designs made of stone. Roman mosaics of stone or glass depict everything from ancient ruins to flowers and wildlife.

The exquisite details found in the micromosaics are so fine they resemble paintings. These are very desirable and sought by stickpin collectors with the better examples commanding higher prices.

SCENIC • *Yellow gold pin and oval mount set with red onyx inlaid with a micromosaic scene of an ancient Roman ruins, mid-Victorian era.* $200.00–250.00.

PLATE 37

TOP ROW *(left to right)*

FLORAL PATTERN • Gold-filled pin and mount set with pieces of colored glass to form a floral bouquet against a black background, mid-Victorian era. $25.00–35.00.

SCENIC • Yellow gold pin and oval mount set with red onyx inlaid with a micromosiac scene of an ancient Roman ruins, mid-Victorian era. (Note: This is the same pin shown in the lead photo of this category.) $200.00–250.00.

PIETRA DURA • Yellow gold pin and oval mount set with pieces of coral, turquoise, and malachite cemented into a black marble background to form a floral pattern, mid-Victorian era. $150.00–200.00.

SCENIC • Yellow gold pin and oval mount set with blue onyx inlaid with a micromosaic scene of an ancient Roman ruins, mid-Victorian era. $200.00–250.00.

PARTHENON • Yellow gold pin and round mount with black onyx inlaid with a micromosaic scene of the famous temple atop the Acropolis in Athens, mid-Victorian era. $200.00–250.00.

SECOND ROW *(left to right)*

RANDOM PATTERN • Gold-plated pin and diamond shaped-mount set with pieces of colored glass to form a casual design to fit the mount, late Victorian era. $25.00–35.00.

FLORAL PATTERN • Gold-filled pin and star-shaped mount set with pieces of colored glass to form a floral design in the center, late Victorian era. $25.00–35.00.

PIETRA DURA • Yellow gold pin and oval mount set with pieces of coral, turquoise, malachite, and jasper forming a floral design cemented into a black marble background, mid-Victorian era. $150.00–200.00.

RANDOM PATTERN • Gold-plated pin and square mount set with pieces of colored glass in a casual design to fit the mount, late Victorian era. $25.00–35.00.

RANDOM PATTERN • Gold-plated pin and teardrop-shaped mount set with pieces of colored glass in a casual design to fit the mount, reverse of mount is marked "EAP" (E.A. Potter & Co., Providence, R.I.), circa 1900. $25.00–35.00.

THIRD ROW *(left to right)*

SCARAB • Yellow gold pin and round mount set with pieces of colored glass in a dung beetle design, late Victorian era. $25.00–35.00.

STAR AND FLOWER PATTERN • Gold-plated pin and marquise-shaped mount set with pieces of colored glass in a random design to fit the mount, reverse of mount marked "800," late Victorian era. $25.00–35.00.

PIETRA DURA • Yellow gold pin and oval mount set with pieces of coral, turquoise, and jasper forming a floral pattern cemented into a black marble background, mid-Victorian era. $150.00–200.00.

FLORAL PATTERN • Gold-plated pin and diamond-shaped mount set with pieces of colored glass forming a design to fit the mount, reverse of mount marked "O," late Victorian era. $25.00–35.00.

PLATE 37

BIRD • Gold-plated pin and round mount set with pieces of colorful glass forming the image of a flying dove, late Victorian era. $25.00–35.00.

FOURTH ROW (left to right)

FLOWER • Gold-plated pin and round mount set with pieces of colored glass forming the image of a flower, Art Nouveau era. $25.00–35.00.

RANDOM PATTERN • Gold-plated pin and teardrop-shaped mount set with pieces of colored glass in a flower and star design to fit the mount, reverse of mount marked "MADE IN ITALY," Art Deco era. $25.00–35.00.

PIETRA DURA • Yellow gold pin and oval mount set with pieces of jasper and coral forming a tulip cemented into a black marble background, mid-Victorian era. $150.00–200.00.

RANDOM PATTERN • Gold-plated pin and triangular-shaped mount set with pieces of colored glass in a casual design to fit the mount, Art Nouveau era. $25.00–35.00.

FLORAL PATTERN • Gold-plated pin and oval mount set with pieces of colored glass in a floral motif, reverse of mount is marked "EAP" (E.A. Potter & Co., Providence, R.I.), circa 1900. $25.00–35.00.

FIFTH ROW (left to right)

FLOWER • Gold-plated pin and round mount set with pieces of green glass circling a white glass flower, late Victorian era. $25.00–35.00.

INSECT • Gold-filled pin and rectangular mount in a black metal frame with pieces of coral, malachite, and jasper cemented in a white marble background, Edwardian era. $100.00–150.00.

PIETRA DURA • Yellow gold pin and oval mount set with pieces of coral, malachite, turquoise, and jasper cemented into a black marble background, mid-Victorian era. $100.00–150.00.

MILITARY, POLITICAL, AND RELIGIOUS

Political items of all types are highly collectible today. Like advertising stickpins, these were giveaway items and were cheaply made. Once the elections had passed, so too did many of the campaign pieces along with the historical events they represented.

Military memorabilia has always held the interest of collectors. Following all wars, as the years turn into decades, such specimens become more rare and more valuable.

As for religious collectibles, they have always been and will always be popular and sought after items.

PRESIDENTIAL CAMPAIGN • *Copper pin and mount shaped like Theodore Roosevelt's Rough Rider hat, brim is marked "ROOSEVELT," only traces of original gold plate still show, circa 1901. $60.00–80.00.*

PLATE 38

FIRST ROW *(left to right)*

SOCIALIST PARTY • Gold-plated pin and copper mount with Socialist Party's red, white, and blue inlaid enameled emblem lettered "SOCIALIST PARTY – WORKERS OF THE WORLD UNITE," reverse lettered "M.P.B. P.I.J." in stamped shield, circa 1912. $20.00–35.00.

CAMPAIGN PIN • Gold-plated pin and mount with right profile bust of a male candidate and lettered "WATSON," Art Nouveau era. $5.00–10.00.

CAMPAIGN PIN • Steel pin and mount with red, white, and blue enameled button bearing the photo images of two candidates and lettered "McKINLEY & CLOUGH," circa 1896. $35.00–50.00.

CAMPAIGN PIN • Gold-plated pin and mount with red, white, and blue enameled oval button bearing etched likeness of Abraham Lincoln, lettered "LINCOLN LEGION," circa 1860. $20.00–35.00.

PROHIBITIONIST PARTY • Gold-plated pin and mount shaped like a hatchet and stamped on the handle with the lettering "CARRY A. NATION," circa 1900. $20.00–35.00.

SECOND ROW *(left to right)*

POLITICAL PARTY • Copper pin with dangling mount in the three-dimensional image of a donkey symbol of the Democratic Party, Art Deco era. $5.00–10.00.

SERVICE PIN • Silver pin and gold-plated rectangular mount with red, white, and blue inlaid enamel bearing a single star denoting a World War I family member was in the Armed Forces of the United States, circa 1917. $10.00–15.00.

SPANISH AMERICAN WAR • Gold-plated pin and stamped thin metal eagle-shaped mount with gold-filled dangling token with raised image of a ship; lettered "REMEMBER THE MAINE," reverse shows flag of Cuba and lettering "CUBA MUST BE FREE," circa 1883. $20.00–35.00.

VETERANS ORGANIZATION • Gold-plated pin and mount with blue inlaid enamel emblem of the American Legion, Art Deco era. $10.00–15.00.

POLITICAL PARTY • Steel pin and pot metal black enameled mount in the shape of a moose and bearing the lettering "BULL MOOSE," the emblem of Theodore Roosevelt's Progressive Party, circa 1912. $15.00–25.00.

THIRD ROW *(left to right)*

NAZI • Gold-filled pin and mount with raised swastika emblem of National Socialist German Workers Party, circa 1933. $20.00–35.00.

VICHY GOVERNMENT • Gold-plated pin and mount with the inlaid enamel black, white, and red colors of Germany and the light blue flag of the French Vichy government above the letters "D.H.V.," circa 1940. $20.00–35.00.

NAZI • Steel pin and pot metal mount with the raised images of a wreath, sword, and swastika, circa 1933. $20.00–35.00.

NAZI • Gold-plated pin and shield-shaped mount inlaid with black, white, and red enameled insignia of a German army division, reverse is marked "Ges. Gesch.," circa 1940. $20.00–35.00.

NAZI • Steel pin and silver-plated mount of two Maltese crosses, swords, and swastika representing military awards, circa 1940. $20.00–35.00.

FOURTH ROW *(left to right)*

RELIGIOUS • Silver pin and gold-plated diamond-shaped mount inlaid with the red and white enameled flaming heart and cross emblem of the Society of the Sacred Heart, probably Art Deco era. $15.00–25.00.

RELIGIOUS • Gold-plated pin and dangled mount of the raised images of Christ and a child, reverse is lettered "SOUVENIR FIRST HOLY COMMUNION," probably Art Deco era. $10.00–20.00.

PLATE 38

RELIGIOUS • Gold-plated pin and thin metal eagle-shaped mount with gold-filled token mount displaying host of Catholic mass, lettered "28th INTERNATIONAL EUCHARISTIC CONGRESS," reverse marked "JUNE 20–24 1926 CHICAGO, ILL.," circa 1926. $10.00–20.00.

RELIGIOUS • Yellow gold-plated pin and rose gold mount in the shape of the entwined anchor, cross, and heart symbolizing faith, hope, and love, probably Art Deco era. $10.00–15.00.

RELIGIOUS • Yellow gold pin and mount of a cross set with nine 2mm rose-cut garnets and a crown inlaid with black enamel and set with five rose-cut 2mm diamonds, late Victorian era. $50.00–75.00.

FIFTH ROW (*left to right*)

RELIGIOUS • Gold-plated pin and dangle heart-shaped mount with microlettering of Lord's Prayer, probably Art Deco era. $5.00–10.00.

RELIGIOUS • Gold-plated pin and oval mount set with the symbol of "PAX," Roman for peace, in black and white mosaic, Art Deco era. $25.00–35.00.

RELIGIOUS • Yellow gold pin and mount in the shape of a cross set with 16 red glass beads, Art Deco era. $25.00–45.00.

RELIGIOUS • Silver pin with mother-of-pearl dangle mount shaped like the Star of David, Art Deco era. $10.00–20.00.

RELIGIOUS • Yellow gold pin and mount shaped in the form of a botoné cross, Art Deco era. $15.00–25.00.

RELIGIOUS • Yellow gold pin and shield-shaped mount with a white inlaid enameled cross on a red background, probably Art Deco era. $10.00–15.00.

RELIGIOUS • Gold-plated pin and mount with marquise-shaped locket and raised letters on the cover "I H S" (I Have Suffered), likeness of Christ on inner page with lettering "SACRED HEART OF JESUS HAVE MERCY ON US," reverse of page shows images of Madonna and Christ Child, Art Deco era. $35.00–45.00.

SIXTH ROW (*left to right*)

RELIGIOUS • Yellow gold pin and cross-shaped mount set with six mine-cut peridots, pin marked "10K," Art Deco era. $50.00–75.00.

RELIGIOUS • Yellow gold pin and mother-of-pearl disc-shaped mount with red inlaid enameled cross, Art Deco era. $10.00–15.00.

RELIGIOUS • Gold-plated pin and mount shaped like a crosslet faced in blue inlaid enamel, Art Deco era. $10.00–15.00.

RELIGIOUS • Yellow gold pin and cross-shaped mount set with 11 seed pearls, Art Deco era. $25.00–45.00.

MOONSTONES

A sacred gem of India, the moonstone is an opalescent feldspar of bluish white. The bluer the stone, the finer the quality. The best examples are mostly found in Ceylon, or Sri Lanka as we know it today. They became very popular as a jewelry item in the late 19th century.

Moonstones were often used by the seers, supposedly giving them the power to look into the future. Legends also tell of their ability to arouse the passions of lovers and to produce a rich and abundant harvest from fruit trees.

Because they are comparatively soft, moonstones are almost always cut in cabochon or in a round bead or ball shape. While carved examples are more difficult to find, they are not uncommon either. They are fascinating gems and are often used in very unique jewelry pieces.

REVERSE INTAGLIO • *Yellow gold pin and oval mount set with a reverse intaglio floral painting in a cabochon moonstone, late Victorian era.* $450.00–550.00.

PLATE 39

UPPER ARCH *(left to right)*

OVAL CABOCHON • Brass pin and oval mount set with a dark colored moonstone, Art Deco era. $15.00–25.00.

ROUND CABOCHON • Yellow gold pin and round mount set with a dark colored moonstone, late Victorian era. $60.00–80.00.

OVAL CABOCHON • Gold-plated pin and oval mount set with a moonstone, late Victorian era. $35.00–45.00.

OVAL CABOCHON • Yellow gold pin and mount inlaid with blue basse-taille enamel and set with a moonstone, mount is marked "14K" with a hallmark, late Victorian era. $60.00–80.00.

OVAL CABOCHON • Brass pin and mount set with a moonstone surrounded by 12 rhinestones, late Victorian era. $40.00–50.00.

OVAL CABOCHON • Yellow gold pin and mount set with a moonstone and a pearl, mount is marked "14K" in a double oval (The Brassler Co., Newark, N.J.), circa 1909. $60.00–80.00.

OVAL CABOCHON • Silver pin and mount set with a moonstone, pin is marked "STERLING," Edwardian era. $35.00–45.00.

OVAL CABOCHON • Gold-filled pin and mount set with a clear moonstone, late Victorian era. $40.00–50.00.

OVAL CABOCHON • Gold-plated pin and basket mount set with a moonstone, late Victorian era. $40.00–50.00.

SHOWN AT LEFT AND RIGHT

ROUND CABOCHON • Yellow gold pin and mount set with a blue colored moonstone and sixteen 2mm rose-cut emeralds, late Victorian era. $250.00–300.00.

OVAL CABOCHON • Yellow gold pin and mounted moonstone surrounded by 24 seed pearls and set with a 2mm single-cut diamond, late Victorian era. $150.00–175.00.

LOWER ARCH *(left to right)*

HEART MOTIF • Yellow gold pin and wishbone mount set with a small heart-shaped moonstone, Edwardian era. $60.00–80.00.

OVAL CABOCHON • Yellow gold pin and mount set with a moonstone, late Victorian era. $40.00–50.00.

JOCKEY'S PROFILE • Yellow gold pin and white gold mount set with right profile of jockey's face carved in moonstone and set with four 2mm rose-cut diamonds, late Victorian era. $1,000.00–1,200.00.

ROUND CABOCHON • Yellow gold pin and mount set with a round moonstone and accompanied with the following documentation "Stone was found at Moonstone Beach, California, March 7, 1920, and was polished and mounted in Los Angeles," circa 1920. $35.00–45.00.

OVAL CABOCHON • Gold-plated pin and mount set with a small moonstone, late Victorian era. $20.00–30.00.

CENTERED AT BOTTOM

CLOVER MOTIF • Yellow gold pin and mount set with three perfect moonstone balls in a cloverleaf pattern, late Victorian era. $350.00–400.00.

PLATE 39

OPALS

Even in the days of ancient Rome, the opal was a highly treasured gem, and it was extremely popular in the Victorian era. The brilliant and vibrant display of fiery colors in this translucent jewel has earned it the reputation of being one of the world's most fascinating of all the semi-precious stones.

Some of the finest examples come from Australia, with the black opal being the rarest of all. It is the quality of coloring found in the opal that governs its appraised value, and appropriately, it is the birthstone of October, the month noted for spectacular autumn colors.

Opals are very delicate stones and are easily cracked or chipped, hence they are usually cut in flat or cabochon shapes. While jewelry items featuring carved opals are not rare, they are not all that common either and are quite desirable pieces.

OCTAGON MOTIF • *Gold-filled pin and Maltese cross motif mount set with a flat-surfaced, octagon-shaped opal, late Victorian era.* $100.00–125.00.

PLATE 40

TOP ROW (*left to right*)

OVAL • Rose gold pin and basket type mount set with a flat-surfaced opal, late Victorian era. $75.00–100.00.

OVAL CABOCHON • Yellow gold pin and basket type mount set with an oval cabochon opal, late Victorian era. $100.00–125.00.

OCTOGAN MOTIF • Gold plate on copper pin and Maltese cross motif mount set with a flat surface octagon-shaped opal, late Victorian era. (Note: This is the same stickpin shown in the lead photo of this category.) $100.00–125.00.

OVAL CABOCHON • Yellow gold pin and basket type mount set with an oval cabochon opal, late Victorian era. $75.00–100.00.

SHIELD MOTIF • Yellow gold pin and gold engraved pentagon-shaped mount set with a flat surface opal on black onyx, pin is hallmarked, late Victorian era. $125.00–150.00.

OVAL CABOCHON • Gold-plated pin and mount set with Mexican opal. This pin was found in its original box marked "THE GEORGE BELL Co., Denver, Colo.," circa 1904. $35.00–50.00.

OVAL CABOCHON • Gold-plated pin and basket mount set with an oval cabochon opal, late Victorian era. $75.00–100.00.

SECOND ROW (*left to right*)

DOUBLE MOUNTING • Yellow gold pin and double mount set with oval cabochon opal above round cabochon opal, late Victorian era. $75.00–100.00.

OVAL CABOCHON • Yellow gold pin and mount set with an Australian black opal, late Victorian era. $125.00–200.00.

ROUND CABOCHON • Yellow gold pin and mount set with a Mexican fire opal, late Victorian era. $125.00–200.00.

STAR MOTIF • Yellow gold pin and star-shaped mount set with a round opal surrounded by five 3mm and ten 2mm rose-cut garnets, late Victorian era. $125.00–200.00.

OVAL CABOCHON • Yellow gold pin and mount set with an opal and two pearls, late Victorian era. $125.00–200.00.

THIRD ROW (*left to right*)

OVAL CABOCHON • Yellow gold pin and mount set with opal and nine 2mm mine-cut amethysts, late Victorian era. $125.00–200.00.

OVAL CABOCHON • Yellow gold pin and mount set with a jelly opal, Art Deco era. $50.00–75.00.

SCARF PIN • Yellow gold pin with gold and inlaid enamel mount set with cone-shaped opal, pin marked "14K" and has hallmark of "Krementz & Co., Newark, N.J.," circa 1894. $200.00–300.00.

INVERTED TEARDROP MOTIF • Yellow gold pin and mount set with an inverted teardrop-shaped jelly opal, late Victorian era. $60.00–80.00.

SUNBURST MOTIF • Yellow gold pin and sunburst-shaped mount set with an oval opal surrounded by 12 seed pearls, late Victorian era. $125.00–150.00.

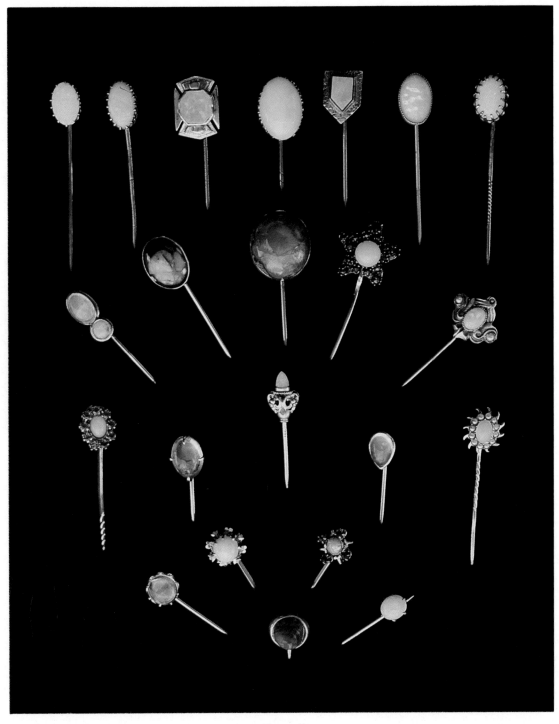

PLATE 40

FOURTH ROW *(left to right)*

ROUND • Yellow gold pin and mount set with a jelly opal, late Victorian era. $60.00–80.00.

ROUND CABOCHON • Yellow gold pin and gold heart and leaf motif basket type mount set with an opal, late Victorian era. $100.00–125.00.

ROUND CABOCHON • Yellow gold pin and mount set with a small opal and four 2mm mine-cut rubies, late Victorian era. $125.00–200.00.

OVAL CABOCHON • Yellow gold pin and basket type mount set with an opal, late Victorian era. $50.00–75.00.

CENTERED AT BOTTOM

CONE • Silver pin and mount set with a cone-shaped Mexican fire opal, Edwardian era. $75.00–100.00.

PEARLS

Often called "Gems of the Waters," pearls are the products of mollusks, such as oysters and mussels, found in the oceans and freshwater rivers around the globe. For many centuries, the beauty of the pearl has been highly valued and much sought after by prince and pirate alike and has been extensively used by the artisans who have created some of the world's finest jewelry.

In perfect orb or kidney-shaped baroque, cultivated or nature's own, pearls have been used to grace a wide variety of items. Even mother-of-pearl, from the milky satin, inner lining of the shelled critters, has been used for everything from buttons and brooches to pistol grips and knife handles.

As may be expected, among the most popular of all stickpins are those set with pearls.

FLOWER MOTIF • *Yellow gold pin mounted with five baroque pearls forming a flower set with a 2mm brilliant cut diamond, late Victorian era.* $150.00–250.00.

PLATE 41

TOP ARCH *(left to right)*

PEARL SLUG • Yellow gold pin and mount set with a pearl slug, pin is marked "14K" with a hallmark, late Victorian era. $35.00–45.00.

BAROQUE PEARL • Yellow gold pin mounted with a baroque river pearl, late Victorian era. $25.00–35.00.

ABALONE • Silver pin and mount set with an oval piece of abalone, mount is marked "STERLING," Art Deco period. $35.00–45.00.

MOTHER-OF-PEARL • Silver pin and floral motif mount set with mother-of-pearl, late Victorian era. $35.00–45.00.

MOTHER-OF-PEARL • Silver pin and mount set with mother-of-pearl, mount is marked "STERLING," late Victorian era. $35.00–45.00.

BAROQUE RIVER PEARL • White gold pin and mount set with a baroque river pearl, Art Deco era. $50.00–75.00.

PEARL SLUG • Yellow gold pin and leaf mount set with three seed pearls, late Victorian era. $35.00–50.00.

SECOND ARCH *(left to right)*

MOTHER-OF-PEARL • Yellow gold pin and custom fitted mount, late Victorian era. $50.00–75.00.

PEARL SLUG • Silver pin and gold-plated vine motif mount, late Victorian era. $25.00–35.00.

HIGH BUTTON SHOE • Yellow gold pin with a mother-of-pearl high button shoe mount, late Victorian era. $50.00–75.00.

PEARL SLUG • Silver pin and gold-plated vine motif mount, late Victorian era. $25.00–35.00.

BAROQUE RIVER PEARL • Yellow gold pin and pronged mount, set with a baroque river pearl, late Victorian era. $35.00–45.00.

THIRD ARCH *(left to right)*

ABALONE • Silver pin and mount set with oval piece of abalone, mount is marked "STERLING," late Victorian era. $25.00–35.00.

BAROQUE RIVER PEARL • Yellow gold pin mounted with a baroque river pearl, late Victorian era. $25.00–45.00.

ABALONE • Rose gold pin and twisted rope dangle mount set with a framed piece of abalone, late Victorian era. $50.00–75.00.

BAROQUE RIVER PEARL • Gold-plated pin and mount set with a baroque river pearl, late Victorian era. $25.00–45.00.

ABALONE • Silver pin and marquise-shaped mount set with a piece of abalone, Edwardian era. $25.00–35.00.

LOWER ARCH *(left to right)*

MOTHER-OF-PEARL • Gold-plated pin and teardrop-shaped mount with one 2mm single-cut rhinestone, late Victorian era. $35.00–45.00.

SCARF PIN • Yellow gold pin and engraved mount set with a single seed pearl, reverse of mount is marked "14K" with a hallmark, late Victorian era. (Note: This stickpin is one of five that was reputed-

PLATE 41

ly owned by Sam Starr, husband of the notorious outlaw queen, Belle Starr.) $75.00–100.00.

LARGE BAROQUE RIVER PEARL • Set in yellow gold basket mount on a gold pin, late Victorian era. $60.00–80.00.

SCARF PIN • Yellow gold pin and mount set with three seed pearls, late Victorian era. $50.00–75.00.

BAROQUE RIVER PEARL • Silver pin and leaf mount set with two single-cut rhinestones, late Victorian era. $50.00–75.00.

PLATE 42

TOP ARCH *(left to right)*

PERSIAN GULF PEARL • Yellow gold pin and a gold leaf dangle mount holding an exceptionally fine Persian Gulf pearl and set with one 4mm brilliant-cut diamond and ten 2mm rose-cut diamonds, late Victorian era. $700.00–900.00.

BLISTER OR MABÉ PEARL • Yellow gold pin and engraved gold mount, reverse of mount is marked "10K," late Victorian era. $100.00–150.00.

LARGE BAROQUE WABASH RIVER PEARL • Yellow gold pin and basket mount set with a baroque pearl from the Wabash River in Indiana, late Victorian era. $150.00–200.00.

KIDNEY-SHAPED PEARL • Yellow gold pin and keystone-shaped engraved mount with six 2mm brilliant cut diamonds, late Victorian era. $400.00–500.00.

LARGE BAROQUE RIVER PEARL • Yellow gold pin and mount set with a large baroque pearl, late Victorian era. $125.00–175.00.

BLACK BLISTER OR MABÉ PEARL • Yellow gold pin and mount set with a black mabé pearl, late Victorian era. $125.00–175.00.

LARGE NATURAL PEARL • Yellow gold pin and mount set with a large perfectly shaped natural pearl, mount is set with 24 tiny rose-cut diamonds, late Victorian era. $500.00–600.00.

SECOND ARCH *(left to right)*

PEAR-SHAPED PEARL • Yellow gold pin and mount set with 12 tiny rose-cut diamonds, late Victorian era. $200.00–300.00.

BEE MOTIF • Yellow gold pin and mount set with a baroque pearl body, 10 seed pearls in the wings, a European cut citrine head, and two ruby eyes, late Victorian era. $250.00–300.00.

MATCHED PEARLS • Yellow gold pin and mount with a pair of matching pearls, late Victorian era. $75.00–125.00.

FLOWER MOTIF • Yellow gold pin and mount set with five baroque pearls forming a flower set with a 2mm brilliant cut diamond, late Victorian era. (Note: This is the same stickpin shown in the lead photo to this category.) $150.00–250.00.

FLEUR-DE-LIS MOTIF • Yellow gold pin and mount set with five baroque pearls, 16 graduated seed pearls, and a 2mm sapphire, late Victorian era. $150.00–200.00.

THIRD ARCH *(left to right)*

SMALL PEARL SLUG • Gold-plated pin and mount set with a tiny mine-cut amethyst, pin is marked "10K," late Victorian era. $35.00–50.00.

PEARL TRIO • Yellow gold pin and mount set with three pearls and a tiny pale blue stone, pin is marked "P.S. &Co." (Plainville Stock Co., Plainview, Mass.), circa 1896. $35.00–50.00.

PINK PEARL • Yellow gold pin and mount set with a pink pearl, late Victorian era. $75.00–100.00.

PEARL • Yellow gold pin and gold filigree mount with a green enamel leaf, three pearls, and seven seed pearls, late Victorian era. $100.00–175.00.

BAROQUE PEARL • Gold-plated pin and mount set with a baroque pearl, pin is marked "P.S.&CO." (Plainville Stock Co., Plainview, Mass.), circa 1896. $30.00–50.00.

FOURTH ARCH *(left to right)*

PEARL • Yellow gold pin and leaf mount with a 3mm pearl and two 2mm single-cut diamonds, late Victorian era. $75.00–125.00.

PEARL • Yellow gold pin and flower motif mount set with a 5mm pearl, late Victorian era. $75.00–100.00.

BAROQUE PEARL • Yellow gold pin and mount set with a baroque pearl and a 7mm mine-cut sapphire, pin marked "H14K" (Heeren Bros. Co., Pittsburgh, Penn.), circa 1904. $75.00–125.00.

PAIR OF GRADUATED PEARLS • Yellow gold pin and mount set with a pair of graduated pearls and five seed pearls, pin marked "H14K" (Heeren Bros. Co., Pittsburgh, Penn.), circa 1904. $60.00–80.00.

CENTERED AT BOTTOM

PEAR-SHAPED PEARL • Yellow gold pin and leaf mount set with a pear-shaped pearl and two 2mm cabochon rubies, pin is marked "14K," late Victorian era. $75.00–125.00.

PLATE 42

⁂ 90 ⁂

PORTRAITS AND PHOTOGRAPHS

As far back as the 18th century, artists were creating miniature paintings – especially for use in pieces of jewelry. The largest of these works would cover no more than the surface area of a brooch, while the smallest examples are probably found set in earrings and stickpins. Even the tiniest of these sometimes exhibited exquisite detail, and those of finer quality, signed by the artist, are the most desirable.

The subjects ranged from paintings of mythological characters, portraits of loved ones, and even scenic vistas. Much of this work was done on ivory or porcelain, although some was applied directly to metal.

While the popularity of miniature paintings continued throughout most of the Victorian era, many of the subjects found in stickpins of later years are actual photographs. A few are quite rare, though the majority are usually valued far less than painted portraits.

LADY'S PORTRAIT • *Yellow gold pin and round mount framing a painting on porcelain of a 19th century lady, mid-Victorian era. $75.00–100.00.*

PLATE 43

FIRST ROW *(left to right)*

SPHINX • Silver pin and round mount holding a miniature painting on porcelain of the famous Egyptian wonder, reverse of mount is marked "800," late Victorian era. $65.00–95.00.

LADY'S PORTRAIT • Yellow gold pin and round mount set with the portrait of a lady painted on a basse-taille enamel background, late Victorian era. $125.00–175.00.

GREEK ATHLETE • Yellow gold pin and wedge-shaped mount holding a portrait painted on porcelain of a young man wearing the olive wreath of victory, mid-Victorian era. $45.00–75.00.

LADY • Rose gold pin and round mount holding portrait painted on porcelain of lady adorned with jewels and flowers, late Victorian era. $45.00–75.00.

MAN'S PORTRAIT • Yellow gold pin and silver mount holding a basse-taille enamel portrait painted on porcelain of a young man, late Victorian era. $125.00–175.00.

SECOND ROW *(left to right)*

CHILD • Yellow gold pin and oval mount holding a portrait painted on porcelain of a female child, late Victorian era. $45.00–75.00.

SATSUMA • Yellow gold pin and round mount holding likeness of a geisha girl painted on crackle glazed porcelain accented with gold metal inlays in the Japanese satsuma tradition, late Victorian era. $75.00–100.00.

GIRL WITH FLOWERS • Yellow gold pin and oval mount set with a full-figured painting on porcelain of a young girl with a bouquet of wild flowers, late Victorian era. $45.00–75.00.

SATSUMA • Yellow gold pin and shield-shaped mount holding likeness of geisha girl painted on crackle glazed porcelain accented with gold metal inlays, marked with Japanese "mon" (mark) on reverse of mount, late Victorian era. $75.00–100.00.

GENTLEMAN • Gold-filled pin mounted with a gilded oval twisted rope designed frame holding a painting on porcelain of an early 19th century gentleman, mid-Victorian era. $45.00–75.00.

THIRD ROW *(left to right)*

LADY'S PORTRAIT • Yellow gold pin and gold plate on copper mount with inlaid enameled painting of lady, late Victorian era. $45.00–75.00.

ARABIC MAN • Gold-filled pin and oval mounted portrait of Arabic man painted on porcelain, late Victorian era. $25.00–45.00.

DUTCH WINDMILL • Gold plate on silver pin and round mount holding a delft painting of scenic Holland, reverse of mount marked "STERLING TOP" and the hallmark "CMR" outlined in a diamond (Chas. M. Robbins Co., Attleboro, Mass.), circa 1892. $25.00–45.00.

SENORITA • Yellow gold pin and gold-plated oval mount with the inlaid enameled portrait of a Spanish lady, pin is hallmarked, late Victorian era. $45.00–75.00.

YOUNG LADY • Yellow gold pin and gold-plated spade-shaped mount with the inlaid enameled portrait of a girl, pin is hallmarked, late Victorian era. $45.00–75.00.

FOURTH ROW *(left to right)*

PHOTOGRAPH • Brass pin and round brass mount covered with brown-tone photo of an early 20th century lady, circa 1920. $15.00–25.00.

PLATE 43

PHOTOGRAPH • Steel pin and gold-plated oval twisted rope mount holding brown-tone photo of early 20th century lady, Edwardian era. $25.00–35.00.

PHOTOGRAPH • Yellow gold pin with a gold scroll mount set with a 2mm mine-cut amethyst holding a round gold framed tinted photo of an early 20th century man, reverse of mount is marked with "SD" and a crossed ax and pike, circa 1910. $35.00–50.00.

PHOTOGRAPH • Gold-plated pin and oval twisted rope mount holding brown-tone photograph of child, circa 1920. $25.00–35.00.

PHOTOGRAPH • Brass pin and round brass mount framing brown-tone photo of a late 19th century lady, circa 1880. $15.00–25.00.

FIFTH ROW (left to right)

PHOTOGRAPH • Brass pin and round brass mount framing tinted photo of early 20th century girl, circa 1920. $15.00–25.00.

PHOTOGRAPH • Brass pin and gold plate on copper oval twisted rope mount holding a brown-tone photo of an infant, circa 1920. $25.00–35.00.

PHOTOGRAPH • Brass pin and gold plate on copper square twisted rope mount holding the tinted photo of an early 20th century lady, circa 1920. $25.00–35.00.

PHOTOGRAPH • Brass pin and oval mount holding the photo of an early 20th century lady, circa 1925. $15.00–25.00.

PHOTOGRAPH • Brass pin and round brass mount framing brown-tone photo of a 19th century lady, circa 1830. $15.00–25.00.

SIXTH ROW (left to right)

PHOTOGRAPH • Brass pin and round brass mount holding brown-tone photo of a 19th century lady, circa 1890. $15.00–25.00.

PHOTOGRAPH • Silver pin and round brass twisted rope mount with brown-tone photo of 19th century man, circa 1880. $25.00–35.00.

PHOTOGRAPH • Brass pin and round brass mount framing black and white photo of a religious painting, circa 1920. $15.00–25.00.

PHOTOGRAPH • Gold-plated pin and round twisted rope mount holding the tinted photo of an infant, circa 1925. $25.00–35.00.

PHOTOGRAPH • Brass pin and round mount framing brown-tone photo of a young lad wearing sailor suit, circa 1920. $15.00–25.00.

QUARTZ

Of all the minerals found throughout the world, quartz is without a doubt the most abundant, versatile, and commonly used in the manufacture of jewelry. The color range of quartz covers every tint and hue of the rainbow spectrum with densities varying from the translucent to the opaque.

As far back as the Stone Age, mankind has been fascinated with quartz, and the ancient Romans used wedges of the pure colorless variety as lenses to reflect the sun's rays. In later times it was discovered that veins of gold were often found in white or milk-colored quartz.

Quartz are fairly hard stones and can be faceted or carved for a wide variety of adornment pieces. Gemstones in this classification are comparatively inexpensive and are used extensively in creating very attractive popular priced jewelry. Most of the stickpins shown here are set with rose quartz.

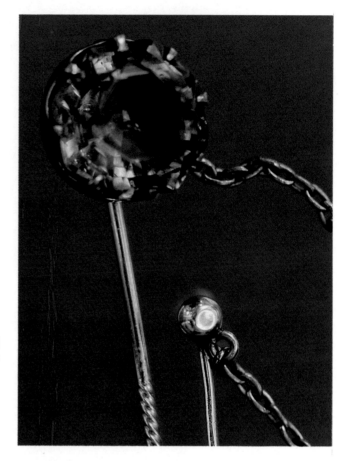

SMOKY QUARTZ • *Yellow gold pin and mount set with a 12mm faceted stone and a gold chain connecting the mount to a gold guard pin, late Victorian era.* $75.00–100.00.

PLATE 44

FIRST ROW (*left to right*)

PINK QUARTZ • Yellow gold pin and engraved mount set with an oval faceted pink stone, pin is marked "10K," late Victorian era. $45.00–75.00.

PINK QUARTZ • Yellow gold pin and engraved mount set with an oval faceted pink stone, late Victorian era. $45.00–75.00.

PINK QUARTZ • Yellow gold pin and 10 pronged mount set with a 13mm oval faceted pink stone, late Victorian era. $75.00–100.00.

PINK QUARTZ • Yellow gold pin and gold filigree mount set with an oval faceted pink stone surrounded by 22 baroque seed pearls, late Victorian era. $65.00–85.00.

PINK QUARTZ • Yellow gold pin and engraved marquise-shaped mount set with a faceted hexagonal pink stone, pin is marked "G L P CO" (George L. Paine & Co. – N. Attleboro, Mass), circa 1909. $25.00–45.00.

SECOND ROW (*left to right*)

DOUBLET • Yellow gold pin and filigree mount set with a marquise-shaped pink cabochon doublet (two pieces of quartz fused together to enhance the color), Edwardian era. $25.00–45.00.

PINK QUARTZ • Yellow gold pin and filigree mount set with a seed pearl and a diamond-shaped faceted pink stone, pin is marked "10K," late Victorian era. $45.00–75.00.

PINK AND CLEAR QUARTZ • Gold-filled pin and swirled mount set with a 2mm single-cut faceted clear stone and two 3mm single-cut pink stones, Art Deco era. $20.00–35.00.

DOUBLET • Yellow gold pin and chevron-shaped mount set with an oval cabochon rose-colored doublet, Art Deco era. $15.00–25.00.

PINK QUARTZ • Yellow gold pin with a filigree and leaf motif mount set with a square faceted pink stone, Art Deco era. $25.00–45.00.

THIRD ROW (*left to right*)

PINK QUARTZ • Silver pin and round silver filigree mount set with a 2mm mine-cut pink stone, late Victorian era. $10.00–20.00.

PINK QUARTZ • Yellow gold pin and white gold hexagonal filigree mount set with a 4mm round faceted pink stone, pin is marked "10K," Art Deco era. $45.00–75.00.

PINK QUARTZ • Silver pin and hexagon-shaped mount set with a 10mm faceted pink stone, Art Deco era. $25.00–45.00.

DOUBLET • Yellow gold pin and engraved silver mount set with a square, beveled, rose/blue stone, pin is marked "ALLCO" (A.L. Lindroth Co., N. Attleboro, Mass.), circa 1922. $25.00–45.00.

PINK QUARTZ • Gold-plated pin and round mount set with a 4mm round faceted pink stone, Art Deco era. $25.00–45.00.

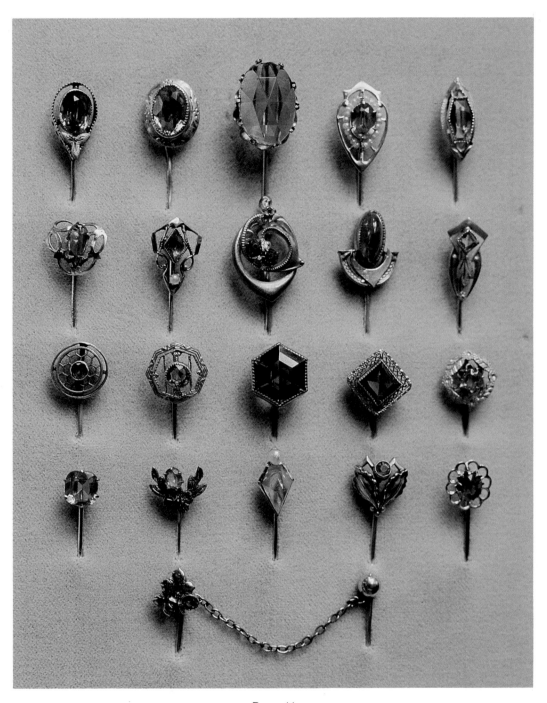

PLATE 44

FOURTH ROW *(left to right)*

PINK QUARTZ • Yellow gold pin and mount set with a 6mm cushion-cut pink stone, Art Deco era. $60.00–80.00.

PINK QUARTZ • Yellow gold pin and floral motif mount set with a 3mm faceted pink stone and a 1mm rose-cut stone in the flower, late Victorian era. $25.00–45.00.

PINK QUARTZ • Yellow gold pin and mount set with a diamond-shaped, pink stone and a single baroque seed pearl, Art Deco era. $20.00–25.00.

PINK QUARTZ • Gold-filled pin and leaf motif mount set with a 2mm single-cut pink stone, Art Deco era. $25.00–45.00.

PINK QUARTZ • Yellow gold pin and filigree mount set with a 5mm brilliant cut pink stone, Art Deco era. $25.00–45.00.

SHOWN AT BOTTOM

PINK QUARTZ • Gold-filled pin and floral motif mount set with a 2mm pink stone and fitted with a gold-filled chain and guard pin, Art Deco era. $25.00–45.00.

RUBIES AND GARNETS

The ruby is the birthstone for July and is found mostly in Burma and India. It is a transparent, bluish or purplish red corundum, very hard and brilliant, and has been prized by royalty for centuries. Large, fine-colored rubies are rare and are valued higher than diamonds.

Rubies are often confused with garnets but are harder and most often display a spectrum of two shades of red while the garnet shows but one. There are also many synthetic rubies on the market.

The garnet is the birthstone for January, and it is found throughout the world. It is more plentiful and valued lower than the ruby. The colors vary but are usually darker than deep red wines. Almandine garnets are a dark purplish red. Pyrope garnets are blood red, while demantoid garnets are green, more rare, and come only from the Ural Mountains in Russia.

RUBIES AND DIAMONDS • *Yellow gold pin and open wreath motif mount set with twenty-one 2mm mine-cut rubies and twelve 2mm mine-cut diamonds, late Victorian era. $200.00–300.00.*

PLATE 45

UPPER ARCH (*left to right*)

GARNET • Yellow gold pin and mount set with a brilliant cut almandine garnet and a small pearl, pin is marked "14K," late Victorian era. $100.00–150.00.

CHERRY MOTIF • Gold-filled pin with a cherry and leaf mount set with two 4mm and eight 2mm mine-cut garnets and scattered pieces of marcasite, late Victorian era. $45.00–75.00.

STAR CLUSTER AND DROP • Gold-plated pin and mount set with eleven 4mm and sixteen 2mm rose-cut Bohemian garnets, late Victorian era. $80.00–125.00.

SYNTHETIC RUBY • Yellow gold pin and Tiffany type mount set with a brilliant cut synthetic ruby, Edwardian era. $100.00–150.00.

HORSESHOE MOTIF • Yellow gold pin and mount set with nine brilliant cut almandine garnets, late Victorian era. $175.00–225.00.

CARVED CABOCHON • Yellow gold pin and crown motif bezel mount set with a rather large, caramel garnet and a 3mm mine-cut diamond, circa 1840. $200.00–350.00.

BUTTERFLY MOTIF • Yellow gold pin and mount set with 30 graduated rose-cut Bohemian garnets, late Victorian era. $80.00–125.00.

FLORAL MOTIF • Yellow gold pin and flower mount set with five 3mm and one 2mm mine-cut almondine garnets, pin is marked with "JM" and other illegible hallmarks, late Victorian era. $100.00–150.00.

OVAL CABOCHON • Yellow gold pin and mount set with an oval pyrope ruby, pin is marked with "14K" and a hallmark, late Victorian era. $300.00–400.00.

SHOWN AT LEFT AND RIGHT

EMERALD CUT • White gold pin and mount set with an emerald-cut ruby, pin is marked with "G14K" (Greenberg & Glaster, New York, N.Y.), circa 1904. $300.00–400.00.

SHIELD MOTIF • Yellow gold pin and shield-shaped mount set with a cabochon garnet, pin is marked "10K-H" (H. Hailparn & Co., New York, N.Y.), circa 1922. $80.00–125.00.

LOWER ARCH (*left to right*)

FLORAL MOTIF • Brass pin and mount set with three 3mm single-cut garnets and a 1mm single-cut rhinestone, late Victorian era. $25.00–45.00.

OCTAGON SHAPE • Yellow gold pin and white gold mount set with an octagon-shaped ruby, pin is marked "10K," late Victorian era. $300.00–400.00.

ROUND • Yellow gold pin and Tiffany type mount set with a 7mm brilliant cut garnet, late Victorian era. $100.00–150.00.

LYRE MOTIF • Silver pin and mount set with seven mine-cut and 17 rose-cut Bohemian garnets, late Victorian era. $75.00–100.00.

PLATE 45

LYRE AND STAR MOTIF • Yellow gold pin and mount set with 13 mine-cut and four rose-cut Bohemian garnets, late Victorian era. $100.00–150.00.

LYRE MOTIF • Yellow gold pin and mount set with four mine-cut and 10 rose-cut Bohemian garnets, late Victorian era. $75.00–100.00.

FLOWER MOTIF • Yellow gold pin and mount set with a 6mm round brilliant cut ruby, late Victorian era. $300.00–400.00.

RECTANGLAR • Yellow gold pin and mount set with a large almandine garnet, pin is marked "14K" and hallmarked with the letter "O" inside a diamond (A.L. Ott, San Francisco, Cal.), circa 1915. $100.00–150.00.

PEAR SHAPE • Yellow gold pin and mount set with a pear-shaped garnet, a single 2mm diamond, and seven seed pearls, the mount is marked "14K," late Victorian era. $125.00–175.00.

CENTERED AT BOTTOM

WORD MOTIF • Gold-plated pin and mount set with 44 mine-cut Bohemian garnets spelling out the word "SKOL," late Victorian era. $100.00–150.00.

MATCHED PAIR • Yellow gold pins and mounts each set with six rose-cut Bohemian garnets, mounts are connected with a yellow gold chain, late Victorian era. $100.00–150.00.

SAPPHIRES AND BLUE STONES

The sapphire has long been regarded as one of the most captivating and valuable of gems. Hailed as the birthstone of September, it is a corundum and second only to the diamond for hardness. The finest specimens are deep blue in color and come from mines in the high Himalayas.

It was thought by some of the ancients that the sapphire possessed special powers to insure good luck, health, and moral character. Occasionally, when the gem is cut in cabochon, it will produce the reflection of a six-rayed star.

Naturally, because of its desirability, many blue stones of lesser value have been referred to as sapphires. As is true with diamonds, rubies, and emeralds, sapphires have long been used in elegant pieces of jewelry – including stickpins.

SAPPHIRES AND DIAMOND • *White gold pin and square mount set with four baguette-cut sapphires and a 3mm brilliant cut diamond, pin is marked "18K," circa 1915. (Note: This pin belonged to Theodore Debs, brother of Eugene V. Debs, several times a candidate for President of the United States on the Socialist ticket.) $250.00–350.00.*

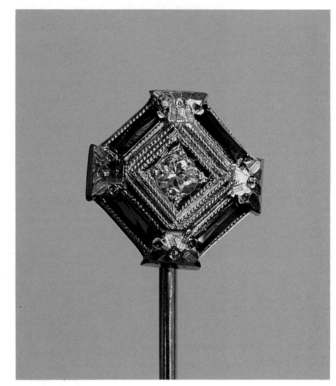

PLATE 46

TOP ARCH (*left to right*)

SAPPHIRE • Yellow gold pin and round filigree mount set with a 2mm mine-cut stone, late Victorian era. $60.00–80.00.

SAPPHIRE • Yellow gold pin with white and yellow gold double ring mount set with 2mm, cabochon-cut stone, Art Deco era. $60.00–80.00.

SAPPHIRE • Yellow gold pin and filigree mount set with a 2mm rose-cut stone and 13 baroque seed pearls, pin is marked "10K," late Victorian era. $75.00–125.00.

QUARTZ • Silver pin and oval mount set with an oval cabochon piece of dark blue quartz, reverse of mount marked "Sterling," Edwardian era. $35.00–60.00.

QUARTZ • Yellow gold pin and engraved mount set with a trillion-cut piece of deep blue quartz, pin is marked "10K," late Victorian era. $45.00–75.00.

BLUE GLASS • Gold-plated pin and scrolled oval mount set with oval cabochon piece of blue glass, Edwardian era. $35.00–60.00.

QUARTZ • Yellow gold pin and mount set with a 4mm, square-cut and a 2mm, round-cut piece of blue quartz and two baroque seed pearls, probably Edwardian era. $45.00–75.00.

SAPPHIRE • Yellow gold pin and engraved square mount set with a 4mm brilliant cut deep blue sapphire, pin is marked "10K," late Victorian era. $75.00–125.00.

BLUE SPINEL • Yellow gold pin and a round engraved and flower motif mount set with a 3mm mine-cut pale blue spinel stone, late Victorian era. $45.00–75.00.

CENTERED WITHIN THE TOP ARCH

SAPPHIRES AND DIAMOND • White gold pin and square mount set with four baguette-cut sapphires and 3mm brilliant cut diamond, pin is marked "18K," circa 1915. (Note: This is the same pin shown in the lead photo of this category.) $250.00–350.00.

SHOWN AT LEFT AND RIGHT

BLUE SPINEL • Yellow gold pin and round mount set with a 3mm brilliant cut pale blue spinel, pin is marked "14K," Art Deco era. $45.00–75.00.

AQUAMARINE • Yellow gold pin and round filigree mount set with a 5mm brilliant cut pale blue aquamarine, pin is marked "14K" and hallmarked with the letter "O" inside a diamond (A.L. Ott, San Francisco, Calif.), circa 1915. $60.00–80.00.

SECOND ARCH (*left to right*)

SAPPHIRE • White gold pin and mount set with a pear-shaped deep blue sapphire and a 2mm brilliant cut diamond, Art Deco era. $150.00–250.00.

AQUAMARINE • Yellow gold pin and a white and rose gold engraved mount set with a 4mm square pale blue aquamarine, pin is marked "10K," Art Deco era. $45.00–75.00.

AQUAMARINE • Yellow gold pin and mount set with a pale blue diamond-shaped aquamarine, pin is marked "G 10K" (O.E. Greenwald, New York, N.Y.), circa. $45.00–75.00.

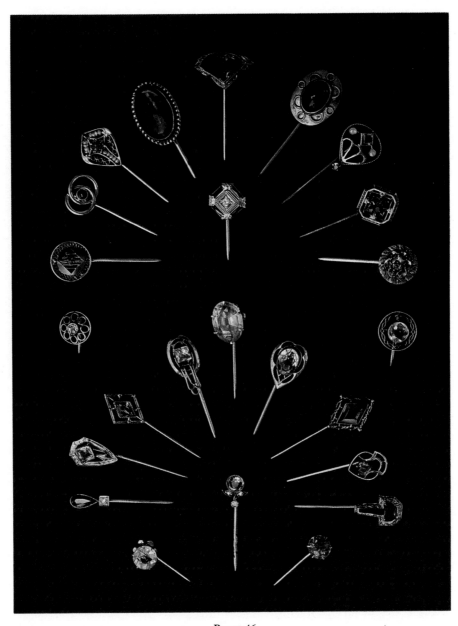

PLATE 46

LIGHT BLUE STONE • Gold-plated pin and mount set with a 4mm square-cut pale blue stone, pin is marked "P.S. & Co." (Plainville Stock Co., Plainville, Mass.), circa 1896. $25.00–45.00.

BLUE TOPAZ • Yellow gold pin and six prong mount set with a pale blue oval topaz, late Victorian era. $100.00–150.00.

AQUAMARINE • Gold-plated pin and pear-shaped mount set with an oval aquamarine, pin is marked "P.S.&CO" (Plainville Stock Co., Plainville, Mass.), circa 1896. $40.00–60.00.

BLUE SPINEL • Yellow gold pin and gold filigree mount set with a deep blue diamond-shaped spinel, pin is marked "10K" with a hallmark, late Victorian era. $45.00–75.00.

SYNTHETIC SAPPHIRE • Yellow gold pin and mount set with medium blue diamond-shaped synthetic sapphire, pin marked "H 10K" (Hayden Mfg. Co., Newark, N.J.), circa 1904. $45.00–75.00.

SAPPHIRE • White gold pin and white and rose gold mount set with 3mm square blue sapphire, pin marked "c.m." (Cheever, Tweedy, and Co., North Attleboro, Mass.), circa 1910. $75.00–125.00.

BOTTOM ARCH *(left to right)*

AQUAMARINE • Yellow gold pin and mount set with a 6mm brilliant cut aquamarine, late Victorian era. $75.00–125.00.

SAPPHIRE • Rose gold pin and round/leaf motif mount set with a 4mm brilliant cut sapphire, a 2mm brilliant cut diamond and two 2mm mine-cut diamonds, late Victorian era. $125.00–175.00.

BENITOITE • Yellow gold pin and mount set with 5mm brilliant cut benitoite stone, Edwardian era. $100.00–150.00.

SIGNET PINS

Probably the most readily available of antique stickpins found by today's collectors are those categorized as "signet" or "initial" pins. The reason for this is simple. Practically every gentleman who wore stickpins owned at least one with a plain surface engraved with his initial(s).

These stickpins came in a variety of shapes and qualities, and wide selections could be found in local jewelry stores and advertised in many popular mail order catalogs of those days. They were fashionable gift items when personalized with the etched initials of the recipient. Some of the more elaborate examples were set with small gemstones leaving a blank space for engraving.

On the average, these pins are found to be relatively inexpensive.

THEATRICAL MOTIF • *Gold-filled pin and oval signet mount engraved with "8 P.M." (arrival time prior to curtain call at 8:20 P.M. at the theatre), late Victorian era. $20.00–30.00.*

PLATE 47

FIRST ROW *(left to right)*

OCTAGON • Yellow gold pin and octagon-shaped mount with an engraved border, not initialed, pin is marked "14K," late Victorian era. $25.00–35.00.

OVAL • Yellow gold pin and oval mount engraved in a floral motif and script engraved letter "E," pin is marked "G L P Co" (George L. Paine & Co., North Attleboro, Mass.), circa 1909. $25.00–35.00.

OVAL • Gold-plated pin and oval mount engraved with Old English letter "R," pin marked "F & R" (F. & R. Jewelry Mfg. Co., Buffalo, New York), circa 1922. $15.00–25.00.

OVAL • Yellow gold pin and engraved border mount set with four seed pearls and raised oval panel, not engraved, pin marked "H A & Co" (Harry Able & Co., New York, N.Y.), circa 1922. $25.00–35.00.

OVAL • Yellow gold pin and engraved border mount leaving a blank rectangle centered for initials, pin is marked "H A & Co" (Harry Able & Co., New York, N.Y.), circa 1922. $20.00–30.00.

HEXAGON • Gold-plated pin and hexagon-shaped mount engraved in a floral and stripes motif and engraved with a script letter "R," pin marked "G L P & Co" (George L. Paine & Co., North Attleboro, Mass.), circa 1909. $15.00–25.00.

SECOND ROW *(left to right)*

OVAL • Yellow gold pin and oval mount engraved vertically with the fancy initials "D R J," late Victorian era. $25.00–35.00.

SHIELD • Gold-plated pin and shield-shaped mount with an Etruscan style border, no initials, late Victorian era. $10.00–20.00.

OVAL • Gold-filled pin and oval mount in scroll, stripe, and notched border motif with plain oval initial panel, pin marked "M M Co" (Moore Mfg. Co., Attleboro, Mass.), circa 1915. $15.00–25.00.

OCTAGON • Yellow gold pin and octagon-shaped mount engraved in a basket-weave pattern with a small rectangle for initials centered at top, late Victorian era. $15.00–25.00.

OVAL • Gold-plated pin and oval mount in a scroll and stripe motif, no initials, pin is marked "G L P & Co" (George L. Paine & Co., North Attleboro, Mass.), circa 1909. $15.00–25.00.

SQUARE • Gold-plated pin and square-shaped mount, rounded corners and a notched border, no initials, late Victorian era. $5.00–10.00.

THIRD ROW *(left to right)*

RECTANGLE • Gold-plated pin and long rectangular mount engraved in scroll motif, long diamond-shaped initial area, pin marked "P M Co" (Providence Mfg. Co., Providence, R. I.), circa 1912. $15.00–25.00.

OVAL • Gold-plated pin and long oval mount overlaid with gold-filled top, set with 2mm single-cut rhinestone, diamond-shaped engraving space for initial, late Victorian era. $10.00–15.00.

MARQUISE SHAPE • Yellow gold pin and long marquise-shaped mount centered with oval blank engraving space, pin marked "P M Co." (Providence Mfg. Co., Providence,. R.I.), circa 1912. $15.00–25.00.

WEDGE • Gold-plated pin and long wedge-shaped mount engraved in a scroll motif with blank engraving space at top, pin is marked "H A & Co" (Harry Able & Co., New York, N.Y.), circa 1922. $20.00–30.00.

OVAL • Yellow gold pin and oval mount with a scroll engraved border surrounding an Old English engraved letter "H," pin is marked "10K," late Victorian era. $20.00–30.00.

PEDESTAL • Gold-washed pin and pedestal-shaped mount with silver heart-shaped blank, engraving panel at top and set with a 2mm, dark blue, single-cut stone at bottom, pin is marked "M M Co. (Moore Mfg. Co., Attleboro, Mass.), circa 1915. $15.00–25.00.

FOURTH ROW *(left to right)*

OVAL • Gold-plated pin and oval mount with engraved border and a blank engraving space, pin is marked "G L P & Co." (George L. Paine & Co., North Attleboro, Mass.), circa 1909. $15.00–25.00.

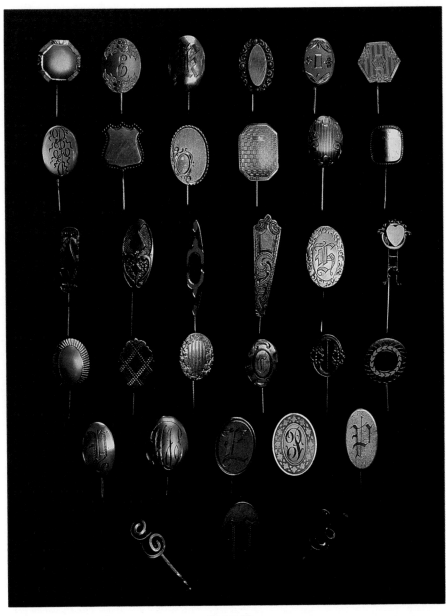

PLATE 47

OVAL • Gold-filled pin and oval scalloped-edged mount with an engraved hatch design and a blank engraving space, late Victorian era. $15.00–25.00.

OVAL • Gold-plated pin and oval mount engraved in floral and stripe motif, blank engraving space, pin marked "G L P & Co" (George L. Paine & Co., North Attleboro, Mass.), circa 1909. $15.00–25.00.

OVAL • Yellow gold pin and etched border mount engraved with an Old English letter "C," late Victorian era. $25.00–35.00.

LETTER • Gold-washed pin and mount in the form of a fancy letter "O," late Victorian era. $15.00–25.00.

ROUND • Yellow gold pin and mount with an engraved and inlaid white enameled border and a blank engraving space, late Victorian era. $25.00–35.00.

FIFTH ROW (*left to right*)

OVAL • Silver pin and oval mount engraved with Old English initial, pin is marked "STERLING" and "A L L CO" (A.L. Lindroth Co., North Attleboro, Mass.), circa 1922. $20.00–30.00.

OVAL • Yellow gold pin and oval mount engraved with fancy script initials "H J S," pin marked "10K," late Victorian era. $20.00–30.00.

LOCKET • Gold-filled pin and hinged oval locket mount with photograph compartments and the front cover engraved with letter "E," late Victorian era. $20.00–30.00.

OVAL • Gold-plated pin and oval mount with an engraved border with the fancy script letter "P," late Victorian era. $20.00–30.00.

OVAL • Gold-plated pin and gold plate on copper oval mount engraved with Old English letter "P," late Victorian era. $15.00–25.00.

SIXTH ROW (*left to right*)

INITIAL • Extruded gold-plated pin with the mount forming the script initial "E," late Victorian era. $5.00–10.00.

OVAL • Yellow gold pin and oval mount engraved with Old English letter "P," pin is hallmarked with letters "A P" (A. Pollard & Co., Providence, R.I.), in an oval, circa 1897. $15.00–25.00.

INITIAL • Extruded yellow gold pin with the mount forming the script initial "E," set with a 3.25mm single-cut piece of red glass, late Victorian era. $10.00–15.00.

SKULLS, TEETH, AND TALONS

As far back as the Stone Age, fangs and talons of wild creatures were used as adornment pieces. Usually these were dangled from a thong proudly worn around the neck as a fetish or a symbol of conquest of man over beast.

In more recent centuries and even today, fangs and claws, both real and replicas, are still used as motifs in jewelry pieces such as brooches, pendants, charms, fobs, and also stickpins. Often these pieces are found set in precious metals and embellished with gemstones.

Some organizations and ethnic groups have incorporated teeth and tusks in the designs of their fraternal emblems. Too, much of the ivory from these sources has been used in carvings of all kinds. While rather grotesque, the human skull frequently became the subject of many such works.

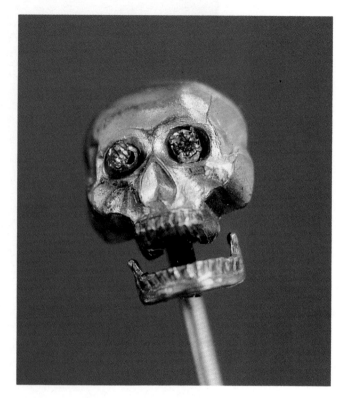

HUMAN SKULL • *Yellow gold pin mounted with a gold replica of a human skull, hinged at jaw, and set with two 2mm single-cut diamond eyes, pin is marked "Pat. March 20, 00," circa 1905. $100.00–175.00.*

PLATE 48

TOP ARCH (*left to right*)

SKULL • Silver pin mounted with a carved ivory skull, late Victorian era. $50.00–75.00.

SKULL AND CROSSBONES • Yellow gold pin mounted with a carved skull and crossbones, often referred to as "The Jolly Roger," a symbol often associated with a pirate's flag, late Victorian era. $50.00–75.00.

IVORY TOOTH • Yellow gold pin and engraved Etruscan-styled gold mount set with animal's tooth, mid-Victorian era. $50.00–75.00.

LION'S TOOTH • Yellow gold pin mounted with the gold capped tooth of a lion, end of cap is engraved in script "M.A.P.," initials of the hunter, late Victorian era. $125.00–175.00.

TIGER'S TEETH • Silver pin and engraved mount holding two teeth from a tiger. The teeth tips are capped with engraved silver matching the mount. India was apparently the source of the mounting, late Victorian era. $200.00–300.00.

TIGER'S CLAW • Yellow gold pin and engraved cap mount holding a tiger's claw, late Victorian era. $100.00–150.00.

IVORY TOOTH • Silver pin and hinged, silver mount holding an animal's tooth and surrounded by eleven 3mm rhinestones, mid-Victorian era. $75.00–100.00.

BILLIKEN • Yellow gold pin mounted with the image of a billiken carved in Alaska from walrus ivory and set with a native gold nugget in its navel, circa 1908. $50.00–75.00.

SKULL AND CROSSBONES • Yellow gold pin and gold crossbones mount holding enamel tinted image of human skull set with two 2mm mine-cut, clear stone eyes, late Victorian era. $125.00–175.00.

CENTERED WITHIN THE TOP ARCH

TEETH • Yellow gold pin and gold chain dangle mount holding three ivory wolf fangs, late Victorian era. $125.00–175.00.

MIDDLE ARCH (*left to right*)

SCARF PIN • Yellow gold pin with the head shaped like a talon clutching a moonstone ball, late Victorian era. (Note: According to a reliable source, this stickpin is one of five that were reputedly owned by Sam Starr, husband of the notorious outlaw queen, Belle Starr.) $35.00–50.00.

TIGER'S TOOTH • Yellow gold pin and gold dangle mount holding a tiger's tooth, late Victorian era. $75.00–100.00.

IVORY TOOTH • Yellow gold pin and mount holding an elk's tooth, late Victorian era. $75.00–100.00.

SHARK'S TOOTH • Yellow gold pin and gold cap mount holding a shark's tooth, gold cap is set with three 2mm mine-cut stones – ruby, diamond, and emerald, Art Deco era. $200.00–300.00.

IVORY TOOTH • Yellow gold pin mounted with an animal's tooth, late Victorian era. $25.00–35.00.

SHARK'S TOOTH • Yellow gold pin and dangle mount holding a shark's tooth, Art Deco era. $15.00–25.00.

PLATE 48

TALON • Yellow gold pin mounted with a gold talon holding a 2mm mine-cut emerald, Art Nouveau era. $60.00–80.00.

LOWER ARCH *(left to right)*

SCARF PIN • Yellow gold pin with a talon clutching a pearl, pin is marked "10K," Art Nouveau era. $60.00–80.00.

CLAWS • Yellow gold pin and mount holding two claws. The mount is fixed with a gold chain and safety pin guard, late Victorian era. $100.00–150.00.

SKULL • Yellow gold pin mounted with an ivory carving of a human skull, Art Nouveau era. $25.00–45.00.

TOPAZ, AMBER, AND CITRINE

The topaz is the birthstone for November. It is found mostly in Ceylon (Sri Lanka), India, Russia, and the United States, with the highly prized, sherry wine colored gems coming from Brazil. However, the colors may vary from gin-clear through yellow, blue, rose-pink, or an orange-brown.

The more plentiful and less expensive citrine is often mistaken for topaz, and it is commonly used in creating very attractive jewelry. Amber may also be erroneously taken for topaz as will some varieties of quartz. The so called "smoky topaz," for example, is actually quartz.

Topaz is easily magnetized when rubbed on a woolen cloth and will pick up tiny pieces of paper. Nevertheless, amber will do the same thing, so this is really not an accurate test. The stones in some of the stickpins shown have this magnetic quality.

TOPAZ • *Yellow gold pin and mount set with a kite-shaped topaz, pin is marked "14K," late Victorian era. $125.00–175.00.*

PLATE 49

UPPER ARCH (*left to right*)

AMBER • Brass pin and mount set with an oval cabochon stone, Art Deco era. $25.00–40.00.

TOPAZ • Gold-filled pin and embossed mount set with an oval shaped stone and four 2mm single-cut diamonds, late Victorian era. $100.00–125.00.

CITRINE • Gold-plated pin and lotus motif mount set with an oval citrine, Art Nouveau era. $50.00–75.00.

CITRINE • Gold-plated pin and wreath motif mount set with a cushion-cut citrine, late Victorian era. $50.00–75.00.

CITRINE • Yellow gold pin and twisted ribbon motif mount set with an unusually large citrine, late Victorian era. $125.00–175.00.

AMBER • Gold-plated pin and mount set with an oval cabochon amber stone, late Victorian era. $50.00–75.00.

CITRINE • Gold-washed pin and mount set with a faceted oval citrine, late Victorian era. $40.00–50.00.

CITRINE • Gold-plated pin and mount set with a faceted oval citrine stone and 20 single-cut rhinestones, late Victorian era. $50.00–75.00.

AMBER • Gold-filled pin and mount set with an oval cabochon amber stone, late Victorian era. $35.00–50.00.

SHOWN AT LEFT AND RIGHT

TOPAZ • Yellow gold pin and a lyre-shaped mount set with an oval topaz and 18 pearls, pin is hallmarked with the letter "O" inside a diamond (A.L. Ott Co., San Francisco, Cal.), circa 1915. $125.00–200.00.

TOPAZ • Yellow gold pin and mount set with faceted oval topaz and four 2mm mine-cut diamonds, late Victorian era. $250.00–350.00.

SECOND ARCH (*left to right*)

TOPAZ • Yellow gold pin and wreath motif mount set with a round brilliant cut topaz, pin is marked "14K" and hallmarked with the letter "O" inside of a diamond (A.L. Ott Co., San Francisco, Cal.), circa 1915. $100.00–150.00.

CITRINE • White gold pin and kite-shaped mount set with a citrine stone of the same shape, Art Deco era. $50.00–75.00.

BERYL • Gold-plated pin and embossed oval mount set with an oval beryl stone, late Victorian era. $40.00–60.00.

BERYL • Gold-plated pin and mount set with an oval cabochon beryl and two 2mm single-cut rhinestones, late Victorian era. $40.00–60.00.

TOPAZ • Yellow gold pin and basket type mount set with unusually large oval topaz, late Victorian era. $350.00–500.00.

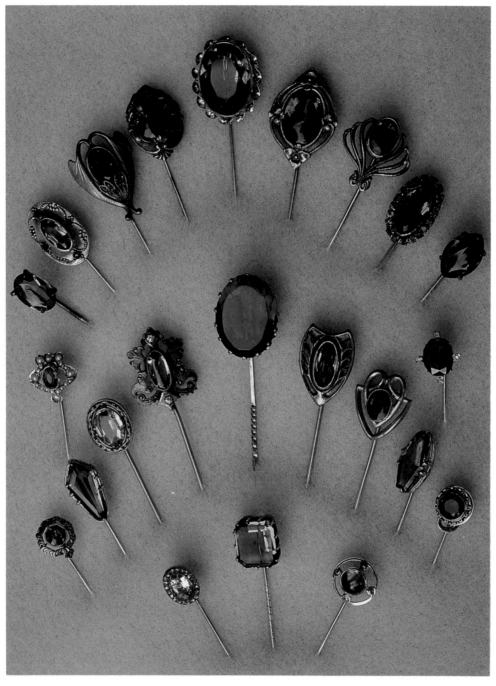

PLATE 49

CITRINE • Gold-plated pin and shield-shaped inlaid enameled mount set with an oval citrine stone, pin is marked "H.A.&Co." (Horton, Angell & Co., Attleboro, Mass.), circa 1919. $40.00–60.00.

CITRINE • Gold-plated pin with a heart and shield motif mount set with an oval citrine, late Victorian era. $35.00–50.00.

CITRINE • White gold pin and oblong hexagon motif mount and a citrine stone of the same shape, late Victorian era. $50.00–75.00.

TOPAZ • Yellow gold pin with a white and yellow gold crown-shaped mount set with a round brilliant cut topaz, pin is marked "14K" with the hallmark of the T.W. Capp Co., of Toronto, Canada, circa 1904. $100.00–150.00.

BOTTOM ARCH *(left to right)*

TOPAZ • Yellow gold pin with a white and yellow gold oval mount set with a faceted oval topaz and 21 rose-cut diamonds, late Victorian era. $250.00–350.00.

"SMOKY TOPAZ" QUARTZ • Yellow gold pin and basket type mount holding a square-cut smoky quartz (often called a "smoky topaz"), late Victorian era. $60.00–80.00.

AMBER • Yellow gold pin and circular mount set with a round cabochon cut amber stone, pin is hallmarked with a clover leaf and "14 K," late Victorian era. $60.00–80.00.

TURQUOISE AND JADE

Turquoise is the birthstone of December with opaque colors varying from light to dark blue or blue-green. The darker blue is the most desirable trailing off to lesser values for the greenish-blue examples showing veins of matrix.

Some of the world's oldest known jewelry was made of turquoise from mines located in the Sinai Desert of Persia (Iran) over 7,000 years ago. These mines are still producing fine quality ore, but the major source of this stone is found today in the southwestern United States, where Native Americans are creating truly spectacular pieces of jewelry.

In the Himalayas of Tibet, turquoise is known as "gyu" which is much like the Chinese word "yu" meaning jade. In this light, while jade is quite different from turquoise, we have taken the liberty of combining the two in the same category.

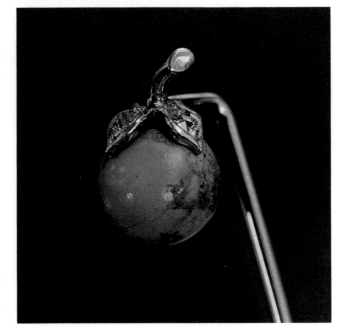

TURQUOISE • *Yellow gold pin and mount forming a branch with leaves and an apple, the three leaves are each set with a 2mm mine-cut diamond, and the apple is a ball of light blue turquoise showing traces of matrix, late Victorian era. $175.00–250.00.*

PLATE 50

FIRST ROW (*left to right*)

TURQUOISE • Yellow gold pin and twisted ribbon motif mount set with a round cabochon of blue, Persian turquoise, late Victorian era. $35.00–50.00.

TURQUOISE • Yellow gold pin and mount set with a round cabochon of blue, Persian turquoise surrounded by 11 baroque seed pearls, late Victorian era. $75.00–100.00.

TURQUOISE • Yellow gold pin and mount set with a light blue oval cabochon turquoise showing traces of matrix, late Victorian era. $35.00–50.00.

TURQUOISE • Gold-plated pin with an engraved gold beaded mount set with a light blue cabochon turquoise showing a band of matrix, late Victorian era. $25.00–45.00.

TURQUOISE • Yellow gold pin and mount set with an oval cabochon of blue, Persian turquoise surrounded by 24 baroque seed pearls, late Victorian era. $100.00–125.00.

TURQUOISE • Yellow gold pin and mount set with an oval cabochon of blue, Persian turquoise stone surrounded by 10 single-cut rhinestones, late Victorian era. $35.00–60.00.

TURQUOISE • Yellow gold pin and mount set with a round cabochon of blue turquoise surrounded by six seed pearls, late Victorian era. $60.00–80.00.

SECOND ROW (*left to right*)

TURQUOISE • Rose gold pin and flower blossom mount set with a round cabochon of blue, Persian turquoise, late Victorian era. $35.00–60.00.

JADE • Gold-plated pin and scroll motif mount framing an oval cabochon of dark green jade, late Victorian era. $25.00–45.00.

TURQUOISE • Yellow gold pin and double teardrop-shaped gold mount set with matched pieces of blue turquoise each showing traces of matrix, late Victorian era. $45.00–75.00.

JADEITE • Gold-plated pin and mount set with an oval cabochon of light green Jadeite, late Victorian era. $25.00–45.00.

JADEITE • Yellow gold scarf pin and mount set with a teardrop-shaped light green stone and a single pearl, late Victorian era. $45.00–60.00.

TURQUOISE • Gold-filled pin and embossed mount set with an oval cabochon of blue turquoise showing traces of matrix, late Victorian era. $25.00–45.00.

TURQUOISE • Gold-plated pin and flower blossom-shaped mount set with ball of Persian turquoise, late Victorian era. $15.00–25.00.

THIRD ROW (*left to right*)

JADE • Yellow gold pin and mount set with round cabochon light green stone, pin marked "14K," late Victorian era. $45.00–75.00.

TURQUOISE • Silver pin and mount set with an oval cabochon of turquoise showing traces of matrix, mount is marked "STERLING," Native American made in the Art Deco era. $20.00–35.00.

JADE • Gold-plated pin and double falcon mount holding an oval cabochon of green jade, pin is marked "P.S.Co" (Plainville Stock Co., Plainville, Mass.), circa 1896. $20.00–35.00.

JADE • Yellow gold pin and engraved mount set with an oval cabochon of light green jade. This pin came from the Weldon Talley estate, late Victorian era. $100.00–150.00.

JADE • Gold-plated pin and floral motif mount holding an oval cabochon of green jade, pin is marked "P.S.Co" (Plainville Stock Co., Plainville, Mass.), circa 1896. $20.00–35.00.

TURQUOISE • Yellow gold pin and mount in a branch and fruit motif set with a round cabochon of Persian turquoise and a single pearl, late Victorian era. $45.00–75.00.

TURQUOISE • Yellow gold pin and an eight-pronged gold basket mount set with a round cabochon of blue-green turquoise showing fractures of matrix, late Victorian era. $35.00–60.00.

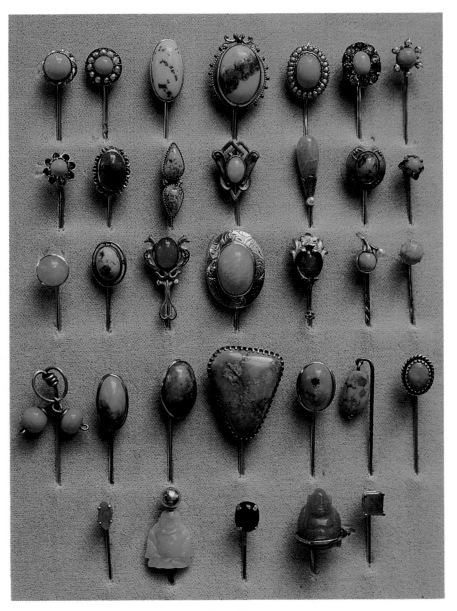

PLATE 50

FOURTH ROW *(left to right)*

ARTIFICAL TURQUOISE • Silver pin and looped wire mount dangling two blue balls of artificial turquoise, Art Deco era. $10.00–15.00.

TURQUOISE • Gold-plated pin and oval mount set with cabochon of turquoise showing traces of matrix, late Victorian era. $35.00–60.00.

TURQUOISE • Gold-plated pin and oval mount set with cabochon of turquoise showing about 50% matrix, late Victorian era. $35.00–60.00.

TURQUOISE • Silver pin and mount set with triangular turquoise piece showing traces of matrix, mount marked "STERLING," Native American made in the Art Deco era. $45.00–75.00.

TURQUOISE • Yellow gold pin and oval mount set with a cabochon of turquoise showing traces of matrix, pin is marked "14K," late Victorian era. $60.00–80.00.

TURQUOISE • Yellow gold pin dangling an oval drop of turquoise showing traces of matrix, late Victorian era. $20.00–35.00.

TURQUOISE • Silver pin and engraved mount set with an oval cabochon of dark blue turquoise, Native American made in the Art Deco era. $20.00–35.00.

FIFTH ROW *(left to right)*

JADE • White gold pin and four-pronged mount set with marquise-cut piece of green jade, Art Deco era. $45.00–75.00.

JADE • Yellow gold scarf pin mounted with light green jade carved Buddha, mid-Victorian era. $75.00–125.00.

JADE • Gold-filled pin and mount set with oval cabochon of very dark green jade, pin is marked "1/20 12K G.F.," Art Deco era. $20.00–35.00.

NEPHRITE • Yellow gold pin and ring mount holding a Buddha carved in dark green nephrite, late Victorian era. $65.00–100.00.

JADE • White gold pin and four-pronged mount set with emerald-cut piece of green jade, Art Deco era. $45.00–75.00.

WISHBONES AND QUESTION MARKS

It is doubtful that anyone knows for sure when the wishbone was first considered a good luck token that supposedly has the magic power of making one's dreams come true, but for untold decades (and possibly centuries), the mystique has prevailed.

As is true with other items such as the horseshoe and the four-leaf clover, the fortunes promised by ownership of the wishbone spilled over into designs of commonly worn jewelry. The stickpin was no exception, and the motif was used in such numbers that these surviving antiques are among those most often found by today's collectors.

While the majority of the pieces in this category will be found to be relatively inexpensive, some have been made of the most precious metals and set with the finest of gemstones.

Almost as numerous are stickpins done in the question mark motifs. The pattern could pose a myriad of queries that could be related to either the wearer or the beholder.

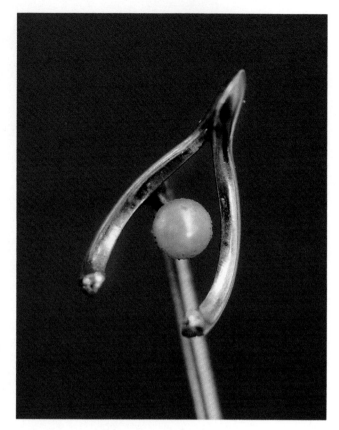

WISHBONE • *Yellow gold pin and wishbone motif mount set with a single pearl, late Victorian era. $25.00–35.00.*

PLATE 51

UPPER ARCH (*left to right*)

WISHBONE • Yellow gold pin and wishbone motif mount set with a 2½mm mine-cut ruby, pin is marked "14K," late Victorian era. $45.00–75.00.

WISHBONE • Gold-plated pin with a wishbone and oak leaf motif mount, pin is marked "W & R" (WHITE & ROUNSVILLE, ATTLEBORO, MASS.), circa 1915. $15.00–25.00.

WISHBONE • Yellow gold pin and wishbone motif mount set with a 3¼mm, mine-cut garnet, late Victorian era. $25.00–45.00.

WISHBONE • Gold-plated pin and wishbone set with a piece of pink branch coral, late Victorian era. $30.00–50.00.

WISHBONE • Gold-filled pin and wishbone motif mount with an inlaid enameled four-leaf clover set with a pearl, late Victorian era. $30.00–50.00.

WISHBONE • Rose gold-plated pin and wishbone motif mount with a yellow gold-plated flower set with an artificial pearl, pin is hallmarked with the letter "F" inside a circle (Stephen L. Folger, New York, N.Y.), circa 1904. $15.00–25.00.

DOUBLE WISHBONE • Gold-plated pin and double wishbone motif mount, late Victorian era. $5.00–15.00.

WISHBONE • Gold plate on silver pin and inverted wishbone mount with an inlaid enameled four-leaf clover, stamped on reverse "STERLING," Edwardian era. $25.00–45.00.

WISHBONE • Gold-plated pin and inverted wishbone mount set with oval light blue glass stone, late Victorian era. $20.00–35.00.

SHOWN AT LEFT AND RIGHT

WISHBONE • Yellow gold pin and wishbone motif mount set with 14 seed pearls and a 2½mm mine-cut diamond, reverse of mount is marked "E.S. 14K" (Ehrlich & Sinnock, Newark, N.J.), circa 1909. $75.00–100.00.

WISHBONE • Yellow gold pin and wishbone set with 11 baroque seed pearls (and one missing), late Victorian era. $25.00–45.00.

SECOND ARCH (*left to right*)

QUESTION MARK • Yellow gold pin and question mark motif mount set with 11 baroque pearls, late Victorian era. $30.00–50.00.

QUESTION MARK • Gold-plated pin and question mark motif mount set with three half seed pearls (and one missing) and a rose-cut rhinestone, late Victorian era. $5.00–15.00.

QUESTION MARK • Yellow gold pin and question mark motif mount set with a brilliant cut sapphire and a pearl, late Victorian era. $45.00–75.00.

QUESTION MARK • Gold-plated pin and question mark motif mount set with nine mine-cut rhinestones, Edwardian era. $10.00–20.00.

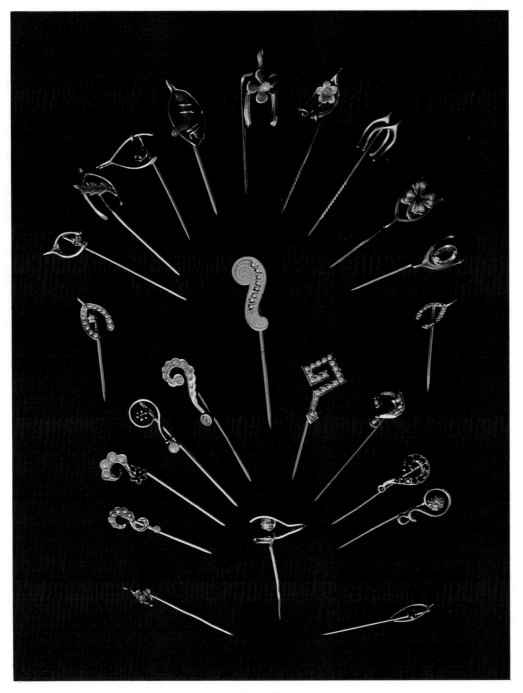

PLATE 51

QUESTION MARK • Gold-plated pin and inlaid blue enamel question mark motif mount channel set with eight seed pearls, late Victorian era. $20.00–35.00.

QUESTION MARK • Yellow gold pin and question mark motif mount set with 18 seed pearls and a 2mm mine-cut diamond, pin is marked "10K," late Victorian era. $75.00–100.00.

QUESTION MARK • Yellow gold pin and question mark motif mount set with five baroque pearls, pin is hallmarked with an arrow pointing to "10K," Art Deco era. $35.00–50.00.

QUESTION MARK • Yellow gold pin and question mark motif mount set with 11 single-cut rhinestones and a single-cut garnet, pin is marked "10K," late Victorian era. $35.00–60.00.

QUESTION MARK • Yellow gold pin and question mark motif mount set with a 3¼mm mine-cut diamond, late Victorian era. $75.00–100.00.

SHOWN AT BOTTOM *(left to right)*

WISHBONE • Yellow gold pin and wishbone motif mount set with three moonstones, late Victorian era. $45.00–70.00.

WISHBONE • Yellow gold pin and wishbone motif mount set with a mine-cut imitation diamond, late Victorian era. $35.00–50.00.

WISHBONE • Yellow gold pin and wishbone motif mount set with a single-cut rhinestone, late Victorian era. $15.00–25.00.

MISCELLANEOUS AND RECENTLY ACQUIRED

In the next four plates, you will find a miscellaneous selection of stickpins that were not in numerical quantities large enough to warrant their own special section, or they are pins just recently acquired after the photography for the book's categories was already completed.

This mixed collection of stickpins presents a wide variety of types, materials, eras, and values. While some are inexpensive novelty pieces, others are counted along with those of our most prized possessions, and a few are quite rare.

Actually, 136 stickpins are pictured and described here, and they probably come very close to being a complete cross-section of examples that span the entire stickpin era from the late 18th century to the present.

CAMEL • *Yellow gold pin and mount shaped in the likeness of a camel's head with a white gold bridle set with four 2mm, mine-cut, demantoid garnets, late Victorian era. $200.00–250.00.*

PLATE 52

FIRST ROW *(left to right)*

ROOSTER • Yellow gold pin mount shaped like a rooster with yellow gold head and feet, baroque pearl body, and single-cut emerald eye, late Victorian era. $175.00–250.00.

AMETHYST • Yellow gold pin and mount set with a 13mm cushion-cut amethyst faceted front and back and surrounded by 19 pearls, mid-Victorian era. $175.00–250.00.

SHIELD • Silver pin and shield-shaped mount with inlaid red enameled botonnée/prefleé cross surrounded by red and blue Old English lettering "XI-HOC-SIGNO-SPES-MED," reverse of shield is marked "STERLING SILVER," Edwardian era. $25.00–50.00.

RED FOX • Yellow gold pin and round gold mount with hand-painted red fox's face on porcelain, Victorian era. $175.00–250.00.

CAMEO • Rose gold pin and silver Etruscan style mount holding left profile of Queen Victoria carved in sardonyx surrounded by red, white, and blue mosaic border, mid-Victorian era. $60.00–80.00.

SECOND ROW *(left to right)*

CAMEO • Gold-filled pin and rectangular mount holding the shell carved full-length figure of a Greek goddess, mid-Victorian era. $60.00–80.00.

CAMEO • Gold-filled pin and oval mount holding a high relief carving of a lady's right profile in pink on very dark red onyx background, late Victorian era. $75.00–125.00.

CAMEO • White gold pin and oval horizontal mount set with chevet carved tigereye cameo in the left profile of a man, pin is marked "10K," late Victorian era. $125.00–175.00.

DOUBLE CAMEO • Yellow gold pin and mount holding the right profiles of a Roman soldier and a lady carved in pink on reddish-brown carnelian, late Victorian era. $125.00–175.00.

CAMEO • Gold-filled pin and rectangular mount holding a six-pointed star carved in sardonyx, late Victorian era. $60.00–80.00.

THIRD ROW *(left to right)*

FLORAL • Rose gold pin and floral motif mount set with three 2mm round opal beads, pin marked "10K," Art Nouveau era. $50.00–75.00.

SCARF PIN • Yellow gold pin topped with a knob of black and white banded onyx, circa 1870. $60.00–80.00.

RUBY • Yellow gold pin with a green and rose gold oval mount in a filigree and leaf motif set with a 3.5mm brilliant cut ruby, late Victorian era. $75.00–125.00.

GOLDSTONE • Yellow gold pin and 14-pronged mount set with beveled goldstone square (aventurine or brown translucent glass flaked with tiny pieces of metal), late Victorian era. $35.00–50.00.

VINE MOTIF • Yellow gold pin with a white and yellow gold mount in the shape of log entwined with blooming vine, late Victorian era. $35.00–50.00.

FOURTH ROW *(left to right)*

GARNET • Yellow gold pin and square white gold filigree mount set with 3.5mm brilliant cut almandine garnet, pin marked "14K" with hallmark of the George Krementz Co., Newark, N.J., circa 1913. $60.00–80.00.

CAMEO • Gold-filled pin and oval mount holding lady's right profile carved in white onyx, late Victorian era. $50.00–75.00.

ITALIAN MAN • Silver pin and silver coin type mount with left profile of man circled with wreath border, reverse marked with raised lettering "G. PURZZI PONTE VECCHIO, 2 FLORENCE," Edwardian era. $25.00–45.00.

PLATE 52

ROSE • White gold pin topped with a three-dimensional ivory carving of a rose, late Victorian era. $35.00–50.00.

RUBY • Yellow gold pin and square white gold filigree mount holding a 3.5mm brilliant cut ruby, pin is marked "14K," late Victorian era. $60.00–80.00.

FIFTH ROW *(left to right)*

FLORAL MOTIF • Rose gold pin with green and yellow gold floral mount set with a 4mm round, cabochon opal, pin is marked with "10K" and the letter "H" (Hayden Mfg. Co., Newark, N.J.), circa 1893. $45.00–75.00.

CLOCK • Brass pin and mount shaped in the likeness of a mantel clock with a swinging pendulum, Art Deco era. $25.00–45.00.

KNIFE • White metal pin and mount shaped like a long curved blade knife with hilt set in mother-of-pearl, Art Deco era. $25.00–50.00.

SHIELD • Gilded metal pin and shield-shaped mount with the raised lettering "I LOVE MY WIFE BUT O U KID," Art Deco era. $10.00–20.00.

CLOVER • Gold-filled pin and mount shaped like three-leaf clover with round goldstone leaves, late Victorian era. $35.00–50.00.

SIXTH ROW *(left to right)*

SCARF PIN • Gold-plated pin and mount shaped in the three-dimensional likeness of a closed lily set with a seed pearl bud, late Victorian era. $25.00–45.00.

DANCERS • Brass pin and inlaid enameled mount shaped like a 1920s dancing couple in formal dress, Art Deco era. $15.00–25.00.

CRESENT WRENCH • Yellow gold pin topped with white gold miniature crescent wrench with jaws holding 3.5mm mine-cut diamond, reverse marked "14K" and hallmarked with letter "C" encircling "Mfg Co" (Cellini Mfg. Co., New Haven, Conn.), circa 1915. $75.00–100.00.

MOONSTONE • Yellow gold pin and ribbon bow motif mount dangling a 4mm round cabochon blue moonstone, late Victorian era. $35.00–60.00.

FALLING DUCK • (Advertising Pin) Gold-washed metal pin and mount shaped like a falling duck, reverse of bird is marked in raised lettering "DEAD SHOT," Art Deco era. $10.00–20.00.

PLATE 53

FIRST ROW (*left to right*)

AMETHYST • Yellow gold pin and mount in a leaf and ring motif set with 3mm brilliant cut amethyst, pin marked "10K," late Victorian era. $35.00–60.00.

ANGEL • Yellow gold pin and round concave stippled mount with the inlaid Raphael-inspired painting of angel overlooking a crescent moon set with five seed pearls, mid-Victorian era. $175.00–225.00.

GARNET • Yellow gold pin and engraved round mount set with a 6mm bevel-cut blood red garnet surrounded by four 2mm rose-cut diamonds, late Victorian era. $100.00–125.00.

AMETHYST • Gold-plated pin and round Etruscan style mount set with a 5mm rose-cut amethyst, early Victorian era. $45.00–75.00.

TIGEREYE • Gold plate on copper pin and concave round mount engraved in a floral design and set with 4mm round cabochon tigereye, a 2mm single-cut ruby, and a 2mm single-cut sapphire, mid-Victorian era. $35.00–60.00.

SAPPHIRE AND PEARL • Gold plate on copper pin and concave round mount engraved in floral design and set with 2mm round cabochon sapphire and 2mm pearl, mid-Victorian era. $35.00–60.00.

DIAMOND • Yellow gold pin and round filigree flower motif mount set with a 3mm brilliant cut diamond, pin is marked "14K," late Victorian era. $75.00–100.00.

SECOND ROW (*left to right*)

RUBIES AND PEARLS • Yellow gold pin with a gold chevron and star motif mount set with three 2mm rose-cut rubies and six seed pearls, mid-Victorian era. $45.00–75.00.

ENAMEL • Yellow gold pin and round Etruscan style mount inlaid with orange-colored basse-taille enamel, pin is marked "14K," mid-Victorian era. $50.00–75.00.

GLASS EYE • Yellow gold pin and round mount framing an iris and pupil of a glass eye, Edwardian era. $35.00–50.00.

GARNET • Yellow gold pin and engraved mount set with a 10mm cushion almandine garnet, pin is marked "10K" and hallmarked, late Victorian era. $100.00–175.00.

ABALONE • Yellow gold pin and round mount set with a round cabochon of abalone, mid-Victorian era. $35.00–60.00.

PIETRA DURA • Gold-plated pin and round mount set with stone inlays in floral pattern against blue stone background, mid-Victorian era. $60.00–80.00.

PEARLS • Yellow gold pin and crescent-shaped gold mount set with five graduated pearls, late Victorian era. $35.00–50.00.

THIRD ROW (*left to right*)

SAPPHIRES AND PEARLS • Rose gold pin and round gold mount set with a 4mm rose-cut sapphire surrounded by eight seed pearls, mid-Victorian era. $45.00–75.00.

HORSESHOE • Gold-plated pin and engraved gold horseshoe-shaped mount with cinch and hinged buckle set with nine Persian turquoise beads, mid-Victorian era. $35.00–60.00.

SCARF PIN • Yellow gold pin and engraved crown-shaped mount topped with a white porcelain ball supported on stone triangles of black onyx, white onyx, bloodstone, lapis, goldstone, and turquoise, mid-Victorian era. $100.00–150.00.

ENGLISH CRYSTAL • Yellow gold pin with an eyelet top from which dangles gold hunter's horn encircling reverse intaglio painting of horse's head in English crystal, late Victorian era. $200.00–250.00.

SCARF PIN • Yellow gold pin and mount designed in the likeness of a king's scepter set with six 4mm cabochon amethyst stones, mid-Victorian era. $100.00–150.00.

HORSESHOE • Rose gold-plated pin and horseshoe-shaped mount set with nine 4mm mine-cut Bohemian garnets, mid-Victorian era. $75.00–100.00.

JASPER • Yellow gold pin and mount set with a cabochon marquise-shaped piece of reddish-brown jasper, late Victorian era. $25.00–50.00.

FOURTH ROW (*left to right*)

FOUR-LEAF CLOVER • Yellow gold pin and engraved four-leaf clover shaped mount inlaid with green enamel and set with a single pearl, pin is marked "14K," late Victorian era. $60.00–80.00.

RUBY • Yellow gold pin and six-pronged mount holding a 7mm oval cabochon of genuine ruby and a pearl dangle, mid-Victorian era. $250.00–300.00.

GARNET • Yellow gold pin and square mount set with 2.5mm brilliant cut garnet and 28 baroque pearls, pin is marked "10K," late Victorian era. $60.00–80.00.

GARNETS • Rose gold pin and mount in the shape of letter "K" set with 20 rose-cut Bohemian garnets, mid-Victorian era. $100.00–150.00.

MOTHER-OF-PEARL AND ABALONE • Yellow gold pin topped with a dangled engraved gold cross on a mother-of-pearl disc backed with abalone, late Victorian era. $15.00–25.00.

BABY'S TOOTH • Yellow gold pin and ball mount dangling bezel holding baby's tooth, late Victorian era. (Note: This pin is documented. Theodore Debs, father of Margarete Debs Cooper, had her baby tooth made into a stickpin. Theodore was brother of Eugene V. Debs, Socialist candidate for President of the United States.) $35.00–50.00.

HOLLY • Yellow gold pin and mount shaped like three green enameled holly leaves set with two seed pearls, late Victorian era. $50.00–75.00.

FIFTH ROW (*left to right*)

FLOWER MOTIF • Yellow gold pin and enameled two piece mount in the shape of a flower set with six seed pearls and a 2mm mine-cut diamond, late Victorian era. $125.00–175.00.

JAPANESE MOTIF • Yellow gold pin and gold hexagon-shaped mount with the grisaille form of enamel depicting a black, gray, and gold landscape scene with Mt. Fugi in background, mount is hallmarked with the letter "M" in a diamond, Art Deco era. $40.00–50.00.

SOUVENIR • Yellow gold pin and mount dangling gold frame holding mother-of-pearl square lettered "BUFFALO 1901," reverse has Maltese cross carved on the pearl, circa 1901. $25.00–45.00.

BEER BARREL • Yellow gold pin and flat rose gold mount in the shape of beer barrel, reverse is engraved in script "FROM ERNST - 6/27/82," circa 1882. $35.00–50.00.

HANGING BASKET • Yellow gold pin and mount shaped like engraved inverted temple basket inlaid with black enamel, late Victorian era. $40.00–60.00.

PALETTE • Gold-plated pin and mount in the shape of an artist's palette engraved with the entwined letters "JFZ" and "'85," circa 1885. $35.00–50.00.

LYRE • Yellow gold pin and mount in the shape of a lyre set with 11 seed pearls, reverse of mount marked "14K" and a hallmark, late Victorian era. $40.00–60.00.

PLATE 53

SIXTH ROW *(left to right)*

LIZARD • Silver pin and lizard-shaped mount set with five single-cut rhinestones and red glass eyes, reverse of lizard marked "STERLING," late Victorian era. $25.00–50.00.

CRESCENT AND ROOSTER • Yellow gold pin and mount shaped like crescent moon and rooster, crescent is set with 12 graduated pearls and rooster is painted in red, green, brown, and gold polychrome enamel, late Victorian era. $175.00–250.00.

BEAR • Gold-plated pin mounted with the carved ivory image of a bear's head, late Victorian era. $35.00–50.00.

PEACOCK • Yellow gold pin mounted with the gold likeness of peacock with ruby eye and inlaid peacock color enameled eye-marks on tail plumage, pin marked "14K," late Victorian era. $75.00–125.00.

FAIRY • Yellow gold pin mounted with the gold likeness of a dancing fairy, Art Nouveau era. $25.00–45.00.

ENGLISH CRYSTAL • Yellow gold pin and mount holding the reverse intaglio painting on English crystal of fighting cock, late Victorian era. $200.00–300.00.

ELEPHANT • Yellow gold pin from which dangles a carved ivory image of a charging elephant, late Victorian era. $15.00–25.00.

SEVENTH ROW *(left to right)*

WINGS • Yellow gold pin mounted with gold spread wings set with a 2mm opal bead and 20 seed pearls, Art Deco era. $50.00–75.00.

CAMEO • Rose gold pin and four-pronged mount holding shell cameo carving of lady's right profile, late Victorian era. $25.00–35.00.

"PIECE-OF-THE ROCK" • Yellow gold pin and mount set with piece of gray stone carved in the shape of Gibraltar (trademark of the Prudential Insurance Co.), Art Deco era. $50.00–75.00.

SERPENT AND SWORDS • Yellow gold pin and mount shaped like coiled serpent and two crossed swords, serpent's eye and sword hilts are set with a total of seven 2mm mine-cut rubies, pin marked "HA&CO" (Horton, Angell & Co., Attleboro, Mass.), circa 1919. $50.00–75.00.

GRAPES • Yellow gold pin and round gold mount holding a round piece of white beveled quartz set with gold grape leaves and five coral grapes, late Victorian era. $60.00–80.00.

PLATO • Gold-filled pin mounted with three-dimensional carved lava bust of famous Greek scholar, late Victorian era. $150.00–250.00.

FOX • Yellow gold pin and engraved gold fox's head set with two ruby eyes, reverse of head marked "14K" and hallmarked with letter "R" above scimitar (Riker Bros., Newark, N.J.), circa 1892. $60.00–80.00.

PLATE 54

FIRST ROW *(left to right)*

BOXING GLOVE • Yellow gold pin and mount shaped like a boxing glove and set with a 2mm mine-cut ruby, reverse of glove is marked "10K" and hallmarked with two shields and an eagle's head and the letters "D&C" (Dieges & Clust, Inc., Providence, R.I.), circa 1917. $100.00–125.00.

BASEBALL • Gold-plated pin and oval mount framing the brown-tone full-length photograph of Walter Perry Johnson standing on a pitcher's mound, lower part of mound is marked "JOHNSON," circa 1907. $25.00–50.00.

BASEBALL • White metal pin and round sided mount engraved with fan centered with raised white enameled baseball, surrounding border marked in relief letters "CHICAGO CUBS WORLD'S RECORD BREAKERS," reverse of mount marked in relief letters "BRUNNER BROS. CO. CLEVELAND, O. pat apd for," Art Deco era. $25.00–50.00.

BASEBALL • Gold-plated pin and mount shaped like a catcher's mitt set with a baroque pearl "ball," pin is marked "STERLING," Edwardian era. $15.00–25.00.

BOWLING • Gold-plated pin and mount in the likeness of a bowling ball and two crossed pins, each pin is set with a 3mm single-cut rhinestone, Art Deco era. $15.00–25.00.

SECOND ROW *(left to right)*

SUNFLOWER • Silver pin and sunflower-shaped mount with silver filigree metals and gold center, Late Victorian era. $15.00–25.00.

BOAT • Yellow gold pin and mount shaped like a rowboat holding an oar, a percussion muzzle loading shotgun, and a dead duck, mid-Victorian era. $35.00–50.00.

GLOBE • Gold-plated pin and mount shaped like a world globe with a blue enameled yoke and gold relief letters "ARCTIC CIRCLE," reverse of mount marked in relief letters "SPORRONG & CO.," late Victorian era. $15.00–25.00.

CANOE • Yellow gold pin and mount shaped like double end canoe, pin marked with "14K" and unidentified hallmark, late Victorian era. $25.00–45.00.

TURTLE • Silver pin and mount shaped like a turtle with a mother-of-pearl shell, reverse of mount is marked "STERLING," late Victorian era. $15.00–25.00.

THIRD ROW *(left to right)*

STANHOPE • White metal pin and round mount set with a small viewing lens surrounded by six single-cut rhinestones, when held to the eye, the lens magnifies a miniature photograph of four nude ladies, Edwardian era. (Note: Named for English lens inventor Charles Stanhope, 1753–1816. The process is still in use today, more than a century following his death.) $75.00–125.00.

FELDSPAR • Yellow gold pin and ball mount dangling an acorn carved from "frost" colored feldspar, Art Deco era. $15.00–25.00.

STANHOPE • Yellow gold pin and mount dangling a barrel carved from "frost" colored feldspar and set with Stanhope lens magnifying six scenes of Niagara Falls, circa 1901. (Note: This type of souvenir was made popular in 1901 after Annie Taylor went over the falls in a barrel.) $75.00–$125.00.

FELDSPAR • Yellow gold pin and ball mount dangling a bell carved from a "frost" colored feldspar, Edwardian era. $15.00–25.00.

BIRD • Gold-plated pin and mount in the shape of flying bird dangling a frosted glass powder horn, late Victorian era. $5.00–10.00.

FOURTH ROW *(left to right)*

DACHSHUND • Gold plate on silver pin and mount shaped like a dachshund dog prancing in the rays coming down from a crown, late Victorian era. $15.00–25.00.

ADVERTISING • White metal plating on copper pin and stamped oval mount centered with a raised bicycle wheel and hub surround by the raised lettering "NEW DEPARTURE COASTER HUB," Art Deco era. $15.00–25.00.

MON • White metal pin and gilded oval mount shaped like a mon with Japanese letters in relief. A mon is a Japanese family crest, Art Deco era. $15.00–25.00.

SHELL • Yellow gold pin and oval mount holding piece of rough exterior of a mussel shell that has been carved to show mother-of-pearl beneath, the unusual carving gives optical illusion of mount being set with a large pearl, Art Deco era. $25.00–45.00.

MONKEYS • Silver pin and mount shaped in the form of the three well-known monkeys, "Speak no evil, See no evil, Hear no evil." Both the pin and the reverse of mount are marked "STERLING," Edwardian era. $15.00–25.00.

FIFTH ROW *(left to right)*

LODGE PIN • Gold-plated pin and mount shaped in likeness of smiling man wearing top hat with white, red, and gold inlaid enameled lettering "GL" circled by the letters "S T K S H T W S," Art Deco era. $10.00–20.00.

KEWPIE • Silver pin and mount in the shape of "Kewpie," the creation of Rose O'Neill, reverse of mount is marked "CMC" and "trade KEWPIE mark," circa 1909. $50.00–75.00.

PET MILK • White metal pin with a dangling miniature Pet Milk can, Art Deco era. $5.00–10.00.

PAN • Silver pin and mount in the likeness of the half-man, half-goat Greek god with the weight of the world in the form of a 5mm pearl on his back, late Victorian era. $25.00–50.00.

ANDY GUMP • Gilded metal pin and mount stamped in likeness of comic strip character, "Andy Gump," Art Deco era. $10.00–15.00.

SIXTH ROW *(left to right)*

SOUVENIR SCARF PINS • Yellow gold pins connected with a gold chain and each dangling a "frost" colored feldspar drop, sliding on the chain is a matching drop set with a Stanhope lens magnifying six views of Niagara Falls, circa 1901. $75.00–125.00.

SIXTH ROW *(center)*

SCENIC • Yellow gold pin with a concave white and yellow gold disc engraved with the view of a lakefront church, a sail boat, and flying birds, Art Deco era. $35.00–50.00.

PLATE 54

PLATE 55

FIRST ROW (*left to right*)

HIGH BUTTON SHOE • Yellow gold pin and mount holding the three-dimensional likeness of a lady's leg and stocking in a high button shoe, late Victorian era. $50.00–75.00.

SLIPPER • Silver pin and mount in the three-dimensional silver filigree likeness of a lady's slipper, late Victorian era. $50.00–75.00.

SHOE • Brass pin topped with the highly detailed three-dimensional wood handcarving of a man's patched and dilapidated shoe, Art Nouveau era. $40.00–60.00.

JESTER'S SHOE • Yellow gold pin mounted with three-dimensional model of a court jester's shoe with a raised pointed toe set with a 2mm mine-cut sapphire, sole of shoe is marked "K18," late Victorian era. $75.00–125.00.

HIGH BUTTON SHOE • Gilded pin and stamped metal mount in the likeness of a lady's leg, stocking, garter, and high button shoe, Art Deco era. $10.00–15.00.

SECOND ROW (*left to right*)

SHOE BUCKLE • Silver pin and silver mount in the shape of a shoe buckle, late Victorian era. $15.00–25.00.

EARLY AUTO • Yellow gold pin and mount shaped in the likeness of an early touring car and driver, circa 1912. $15.00–25.00.

SOMBRERO • Silver pin and engraved three-dimensional mount shaped like a Mexican sombrero, reverse is stamped "STERLING 0925," Art Deco era. $15.00–25.00.

EARLY AUTO • Yellow gold pin and mount in the likeness of an early roadster of the Stutts Bearcat design being driven down a dirt road, circa 1921. $35.00–50.00.

PARASOL • Silver pin with silver and yellow gold mount shaped in the likeness of an open umbrella, Edwardian era. $15.00–25.00.

THIRD ROW (*left to right*)

SHIP'S WHEEL • Yellow gold pin and revolving ship's wheel mount, both pin and reverse of mount are marked "18ct," late Victorian era. $100.00–125.00.

TABLESPOON • Yellow gold pin and mount shaped like a tablespoon with the bowl holding a 2mm pearl, late Victorian era. $40.00–60.00.

FRYING PAN • Copper pin and three-dimensional mount of a skillet with the raised head of an American bison circled with "* PAN AMERICAN 1901 *" (Pan American Exposition at Buffalo, N.Y.), handle is marked "pat'd," circa 1901. $25.00–50.00.

SMOKER'S PIPE • Yellow gold pin mounted with a gold and brown enameled three-dimensional smoker's pipe with a 3mm pearl set in the bowl, late Victorian era. $35.00–50.00.

SPROCKET • Silver pin with a silver mount shaped like a bicycle sprocket, crank, and revolving pedal, Art Deco era. $25.00–45.00.

FOURTH ROW (*left to right*)

MOUTHPIECE • Brass pin and three-dimensional mount of the mouthpiece from a musician's horn, Art Deco era. $10.00–20.00.

LIGHT BULB • Brass pin with brass and milk glass three-dimensional mount shaped like a light bulb, Art Deco era. $10.00–15.00.

MOUTHPIECE • Brass pin with a brass and black enameled mount in the three-dimensional likeness of an old telephone mouthpiece, reverse of mount is marked "MONARCH CHICAGO," Art Deco era. $15.00–25.00.

SPOOL AND THREAD • Gold-filled pin and mount shaped in the three-dimensional likeness of a spool holding coils of rope, Art Deco era. $25.00–35.00.

FIFTH ROW (*left to right*)

RAZOR AND MUG • White gold pin with a white and yellow gold mount shaped like a straight razor and shaving mug, Art Deco era. $25.00–35.00.

SAW • Yellow gold pin and mount shaped like handsaw with engraved handle and a blade inlaid with mother-of-pearl, Art Deco era. $20.00–35.00.

TIRE PUMP • Silver pin and three-dimensional silver and copper mount shaped like a stirrup type tire pump, Art Deco era. $35.00–50.00.

SOLDERING IRON • Gold-filled pin and mount in the three-dimensional shape of a tinner's soldering iron, Art Deco era. $10.00–20.00.

SCOOP • Yellow gold pin and silver mount shaped like a miller's grain scoop with a mother-of-pearl handle, Art Deco era. $15.00–25.00.

SIXTH ROW (*left to right*)

MAN'S BOOT • Yellow gold pin dangling a three-dimensional pair of man's hob-nail boots made of blackened metal, Art Deco era. $20.00–35.00.

CANE • Black enameled yellow gold pin and engraved gold handle forming a gentleman's walking cane, Edwardian era. $10.00–20.00.

DOG • Copper pin mounted with the three-dimensional molded head of a black dog with a ring in his mouth, rear of dog's head is set with a 6mm cabochon opal, late Victorian era. $35.00–50.00.

CANE • Yellow gold pin and mother-of-pearl handle forming a gentleman's walking cane, Edwardian era. $10.00–20.00.

SHOES • Gold-filled pin dangling a fully three-dimensional pair of lady's high button shoes made of blackened metal, Art Deco era. $20.00–35.00.

PLATE 55

STICKPIN HOLDERS

Just as ladies of the late Victorian era displayed their hat pins in holders for easy selection on their dressing tables, so too, did the gentlemen of the era keep his tie pins. Both holders were, for the most part, made of ceramics, the difference being that the stickpin holder was much smaller to accommodate the shorter stems.

Since those bygone years, stickpin holders have become even harder to come by than the pins they once held. Many were discarded before the end of the Art Deco era when tie-clips and tie-tacks became popular and the old stickpins were stashed away in some remote corner of a drawer.

Then too, due to the delicate material from which the holders were made, many were broken accidentally. Thus, the supply of these antique pieces has dwindled considerably, and some are now quite rare, driving up the prices today's collectors must expect to pay.

Since these holders are usually sold by those whose expertise involves china and ceramics rather than jewelry, we have not attempted to list their values other than to estimate their current prices would range from about $75.00 to several hundred dollars each.

PLATE 56

SHOWN ON TOP BOOK (left to right)

HOLDER WITH CLUTCH TRAY • Porcelain, 1½" H x 2" W, floral pattern, bottom marked "O&EG" and the word "ROYAL" circled with wreath, followed by "AUSTRIA" (Oscar & Edgar Gutherz Mfgs., Altrohlau, Bohemia), circa 1899.

HOLDER WITH CLUTCH TRAY • Porcelain, 1¼" H x 3" W, rose pattern with gold edgings, bottom marked "PRUSSIA" across a fleur-de-lis, late Victorian era.

SHOWN ON SECOND BOOK (left to right)

BOTTLE-SHAPED HOLDER • Carved from bog oak, 2⅝" H x 1" W, black with shamrocks, it has no markings but was made in Ireland, late Victorian era.

HOLDER WITH CLUTCH TRAY • Porcelain, 1⅝" H x 1", floral pattern with gold edgings, bottom marked "Hand Painted" with the letter "M" circled with a wreath followed by "NIPPON," late Victorian era.

SHOWN ON THIRD BOOK (left to right)

BUD VASE SHAPE • Porcelain, 1¾" H x 1¼" W, floral pattern with gold top, no markings, probably late Victorian era.

BOTTOM ROW (left to right)

HOLDER • Porcelain, 1½" H x 2" W, rose pattern with gold accents, no markings, probably late Victorian era.

SHOE • Porcelain, 1⅝" H x 3¾" L, wild rose pattern with gold edgings, bottom is marked "B&H LIMOGES FRANCE," late Victorian era.

HOLDER WITH CLUTCH TRAY • 1⅝" H x 2⅛" W, rose pattern with gold edgings and accents, bottom marked "HAND PAINTED" and "NIPPON" under a leaf, late Victorian era.

HOLDER WITH CLUTCH TRAY • 2⅛" H x 2⅛" W, in purple and white spring beauty floral pattern with gold edging, bottom of base shows the mold mark "374," late Victorian era.

CASES

Just as a nice piece of jewelry comes in a gift box or a lined case when purchased from a dealer today, so too, did stickpins for the gentlemen of the past. Usually, the more valuable the piece, the more elaborate the box or case.

Some of the antique stickpins collectors chance upon today may still be found in their original boxes and some even in fitted leather cases. Often though the pins have been switched with others and are not those the boxes first held. When they are, though, an added bit of historic information is often provided the collector, for many will be marked on the inner lid with the name and address of the jeweler who made and/or sold the pin.

When a case is found today, it will more than likely be priced and sold together with the stickpin it holds – original or not. If it can be authenticated that the pin and case are actually a matched set, then you may expect to pay a little more for the stickpin, but the difference is negligible.

PLATE 57

SHOWN FROM LEFT TO RIGHT

BLUE VELVET • Rectangular case lined with felt and silk, inside of lid is marked with the jewelry dealer's "K" wreath encircled trade mark and his name and address "ALBERT H. KULL, Jeweler, 142 East Main Street, Columbus, Ohio." The stickpin shown is described in the amethyst category.

MAROON LEATHER • Fitted leather case (closed) embossed in gold accents, interior is lined with felt and silk but is unmarked.

MAROON LEATHER • Fitted leather case with embossed gold trim on outside lid, interior is lined with blue velvet and silk marked with a gold crown and lettering "SKINNER Silversmith and Diamond Setter, Orchard Street, LONDON." The stickpin shown is described in the cameo category.

GREEN VELVET • Rectangular case lined with felt and silk, inside of lid is marked with the jewelry dealer's initial "H" in a shield held by a flying dragon and his name and address "Harry A. Hulett, Jeweler, Marshall, Mich." The stickpin shown is described in the horseshoe category.

CLUTCHES

The most important accessory a stickpin owner can own is a clutch. It is an aid in preventing loss of a valuable piece of jewelry, and it is a safety device to keep the wearer from being pricked by the sharp pointed pin.

Prior to the time when clutches, of the type shown here, were made, several other methods were used to detour the highly polished shaft of the stickpins from sliding through the material causing the pin to become lost. In the Georgian era, for example, many of the pins were bent in a series of waves to help hold it in place. Later, during the Victorian eras, some pins had an additional prong at the top to prevent them from slipping upward. The stems of others were sometimes square and twisted rather than being round.

With the coming of the clutch, practically every stickpin purchased from a jeweler came with its own clutch. Because they were small and removable, many were lost, and the majority of stickpins found by today's collectors are without clutches. Whether the pin comes with or without a clutch seldom has any effect on its value or asking price, and by themselves, clutches are usually very inexpensive.

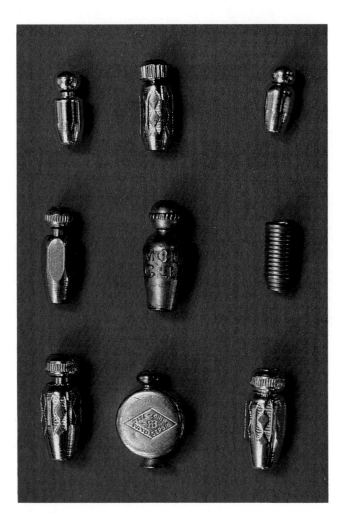

PLATE 58

FIRST ROW *(left to right)*

CLUTCH • Yellow gold plain barrel shaped, late Victorian era.

CLUTCH • Silver hexagon sided barrel clutch engraved in diamond patterns, late Victorian era.

CLUTCH • Yellow gold plain barrel clutch, late Victorian era.

SECOND ROW *(left to right)*

CLUTCH • Silver, plain hexagon sided barrel clutch, late Victorian era.

CLUTCH • Gold-filled plain barrel clutch, side is stamped "MODERN CLUTCH," probably Edwardian or Art Deco era.

CLUTCH • Brass, rubber filled coil string clutch, probably Edwardian or Art Deco Era.

THIRD ROW *(left to right)*

CLUTCH • Silver, hexagon sided barrel clutch, sides engraved in diamond patterns, late Victorian era.

CLUTCH • Yellow gold, round shaped clutch with spring and ball on left and right sides of interior chamber, side of clutch is marked with a diamond lettered "TITE-GRIP RB PATD SEP 5 '16" (Randel & Beremore, New York, NY), circa 1916.

CLUTCH • Yellow gold, hexagon sided barrel clutch, sides engraved in diamond patterns, late Victorian era.

WHERE TO FIND ANTIQUE STICKPINS

Since the early 1960s, when Pet first began collecting antique stickpins, she has found them in about every source imaginable. Naturally, the first places she tried were the local antique dealers, where she made her first purchases some of which were very nice collectibles.

Next came the church bazaars and garage sales that turned up a few pins but seldom anything unusual. Then she checked out the pawn shops and some of the older jewelry stores that had been in business for many years. Here, though the numerical selections were limited, she found some especially fine pieces.

When the supplies of local area sources were exhausted, she turned to the antique shows and larger flea markets in other nearby cities. These sources have yielded the majority of the stickpins in her collection. However, there were other markets to be explored, so during our business and vacation travels, Pet never fails to call on the antique dealers and estate jewelers in the cities we visit.

Additionally, through advertisements in some of the leading magazines featuring fine antiques, she has made contacts that have produced some of her rarest and most outstanding stickpins of all. It is also here that she discovered many exquisite and desirable pieces that she would dearly love to own but simply could not afford.

Collecting stickpins, however, is a hobby for people of any means. Interesting examples can be found priced from a few dollars to many thousands. The challenge lies in the continual search, and the occasional finding, of that old and wonderful hidden treasure that will fit your pocketbook. There are many such pieces out there just waiting to be discovered, and that is what collecting is all about.

Below is a partial listing of sources from which Pet has purchased antique stickpins of all types and values. There are many, many more just too numerous to mention.

AABX Antiques, Clearwater, FL
Amedee Antiques & Estate Jewelry, St. Louis, MO
Baytree Antiques, Peggy Polk, Micanopy, FL
The Boll Weevil Antiques, Calvert, TX
Braun Galleries, St. Louis, MO
The Briars Antiques, Diane Grimes, Olney, MD
Delectable Collectables, Monica Beth Fowler, Micanopy, FL
Knightsbridge, Inc., Earl De Vandekar, New York, NY
Ellen Ellis Antiques, Ft. Mitchell, KY
Famous-Barr, St. Louis, MO
Paul J. Fischer Antiques, Indianapolis, IN
Frontenac Antiques Mkt., Frontenac, MO
Isaac's Gallery, Louisville, KY
Arthur Guy Kaplan Antique Jewelry, Baltimore, MD
Larkin Antiques, Nashville, TN
Marshall Field & Co., Chicago, IL
S.J. Phillips, Ltd., London, England
Dick Robeson Antiques, Zionsville, IN
Silverman Galleries, Alexandria, VA
Mary Spoerle Antiques, Indianapolis, IN
Mary Twigg Antiques & Estate Jewelry, Marysville, OH
Walton's Antique and Estate Jewelry, Franklin, TN
Wayside Antiques & Christmas Center, Reddick, FL
Edith Weber & Co., New York, NY
Don Williams Antiques, Kirksville, MO
George D. Wright Enterprizes, Indianapolis, IN
Gloria Wright Antiques, Indianapolis, IN

THE AUTHOR AND THE COLLECTOR

THE AUTHOR –
Jack Kerins, is a Marine veteran of World War II and a graduate of Indiana State University in Terre Haute, Indiana. He is now a freelance outdoor writer, photographer, and book author.

THE COLLECTOR –
Elynore Petyo "Pet" Kerins, is also a graduate of Indiana State where she and Jack met. She is now a retired speech/language pathologist.

THE COUPLE –
They still make their residence in Terre Haute, when not visiting their three children and six grandchildren. In their travels, they are constantly in search of those rare or unusual antique stickpins to add to Pet's collection.

Schroeder's ANTIQUES Price Guide

. . . is the #1 best-selling antiques & collectibles value guide on the market today, and here's why . . .

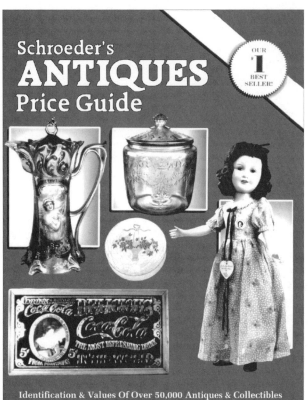

Schroeder's ANTIQUES Price Guide

OUR #1 BEST SELLER!

Identification & Values Of Over 50,000 Antiques & Collectibles

8½ x 11, 608 Pages, $12.95

• More than 300 advisors, well-known dealers, and top-notch collectors work together with our editors to bring you accurate information regarding pricing and identification.

• More than 45,000 items in almost 500 categories are listed along with hundreds of sharp original photos that illustrate not only the rare and unusual, but the common, popular collectibles as well.

• Each large close-up shot shows important details clearly. Every subject is represented with histories and background information, a feature not found in any of our competitors' publications.

• Our editors keep abreast of newly developing trends, often adding several new categories a year as the need arises.

If it merits the interest of today's collector, you'll find it in *Schroeder's*. And you can feel confident that the information we publish is up to date and accurate. Our advisors thoroughly check each category to spot inconsistencies, listings that may not be entirely reflective of market dealings, and lines too vague to be of merit. Only the best of the lot remains for publication.

Without doubt, you'll find
SCHROEDER'S ANTIQUES PRICE GUIDE
the only one to buy for
reliable information and values.

COLLECTOR BOOKS
A Division of Schroeder Publishing Co., Inc.